THE REALIST IMAGE IN SOCIAL SCIENCE

Also by Derek Layder
STRUCTURE, INTERACTION AND SOCIAL THEORY

The Realist Image in Social Science

DEREK LAYDER

Lecturer in Sociology
University of Leicester

MACMILLAN

First published 1990

Published by
THE MACMILLAN PRESS LTD
Houndmills, Basingstoke, Hampshire RG21 2XS
and London
Companies and representatives
throughout the world

Phototypeset by Input Typesetting Ltd, London
Printed in Hong Kong

British Library Cataloguing in Publication Data
Layder, Derek
The realist image in social science
1. Social science. Theories
I. Title
300′.1

ISBN 0–333–49967–0

For Sharon Higson

Contents

List of Figures

Acknowledgements

The greater part of this book was written while I was Academic Visitor in the Department of Sociology, University of New England, New South Wales. I would like to thank the department as a whole for providing such a congenial atmosphere in which to work. In particular I would like to thank Stewart Clegg for his enthusiasm and intellectual support during my stay. I would also like to thank Lance Workman, Margo Huxley, Ian Davidson and Bill Noble for their friendship and help during my stay in Australia.

In various ways the following have all contributed to my thinking about the problems and issues raised in this book; Paul Secord, John Wilson, Terry Johnson, Chris Dandeker, Jennifer Platt, Ronald Frankenberg and Ian Jarvie. I would like to express my gratitude to them all, although they do not all agree with what I say. In this respect they cannot be blamed for pointing me in the direction I have taken!

I owe a special debt of gratitude to Sharon Higson who has supported me unflinchingly throughout the writing of this book and has also lent assistance in preparing the typescript.

Parts of chapters 2 and 3 first appeared in *Philosophy of the Social Sciences* in 1985 and appear by permission of the editors and the publisher Wilfred Laurier University Press. Part of chapter 4 appeared in *The Sociological Review* in 1988 and appears by permission of the editors and the publisher Routledge. Part of chapter 6 appeared in *Journal for the Theory of Social Behaviour* in 1982 and appears by permission of the editors and the publisher Basil Blackwell. Sections of chapters 3 and 5 have appeared in Volumes Eight and Nine of *Current Perspectives in Social Theory* and appear by permission of the editors and the publisher JAI Press.

Derek Layder

Introduction

I view this book primarily as a work in the philosophy of social science, particularly as it applies to sociology and social psychology. Perhaps unusually, it is written by someone trained as a sociologist who has always been interested in philosophical problems and psychological issues as they bear upon human existence and social life. Although the greater part of the book does not *directly* concern itself with issues that confront research-oriented social scientists, nevertheless, what I have to say does impinge on these concerns in a no less important way than a book which concentrates exclusively on practical issues of method and data collection.

It may seem odd to those whose interests lie almost exclusively in the empirical domain that a trained sociologist whose doctoral dissertation contained a sizeable chunk of what is conventionally thought of as empirical research (Layder 1976), should say that they feel totally at ease with many philosophical ideas. However, the fact is that I do. Moreover, I view them positively, and far from being a threat to the practice of social research, I feel strongly that the tackling of certain philosophical problems is an essential prerequisite of adequate and informed social research. To add further to the consternation of those who think of philosophical concerns as heretical, even almost a betrayal of the social scientific cause, I would also claim that there is a realm of philosophical ideas which cannot be adjudicated in empirical terms, that is, by appeal to empirical evidence. However, I would go on to say that there is no incompatibility between a belief in this and the belief that social research is an indispensable aspect of the cumulative growth of knowledge of the empirical 'substance' of the social world.

In the light of these comments it will come as no surprise that I see the relationship between the disciplines of philosophy, sociology and social psychology (and of course the other social sciences, although I do not deal with them in this book), as essentially one in which a constructive and co-operative dialogue can, and should, take place. It is a sad fact that for many social scientists (although by no means all) this kind of openness of approach at best smacks of the possibility of contamination of their own pristine academic area by alien and subversive influences. At its worst it constitutes a direct threat to the indisputable foundations (or, more appositely, 'sacred

1

dogmas') of their own disciplines. Occasionally, individuals of either of these hues will take it upon themselves to attempt to rid their home discipline of such threats to the disciplinary orthodoxy.

The whole thrust of this book is to challenge these defensive postures and to characterise them as attempts to hinder the free and cumulative growth of knowledge in the social sciences. Entrenched dogmas about the necessity for the maintenance of the purity of social scientific disciplines in an attempt to pre-empt incursions from philosophy must be resisted just as vehemently as claims about philosophical preeminence in social analysis (see Winch 1963). This book attempts to steer a course between both of these extremes of disciplinary imperialism which, I believe, can only hinder a more sophisticated understanding of the nature of the practice of social science. Such preliminaries may seem unnecessary to those philosophers of social science who already understand the necessity for a deeper understanding of the infrastructure of social science and social research, but it would be entirely naive to think that this is a view which is commonly shared by practicing social scientists.

The position is complicated by the fact that many practitioners see themselves as possessing a fair degree of sophistication in such matters, or at least enough to do the job successfully and efficiently. As part of this assumed sophistication such practitioners view terms like 'empiricism' or 'positivism' as vacuous and only of use in a stigmatising game of name-calling where the things or activities that are so labelled are, henceforward, regarded as irredeemably 'bad' or 'unscientific' (or whatever derogatory epithet most suits).

This is a most naive doctrine which is as dangerous as it is confused. The confusion arises perhaps because in some cases terms such as empiricism or positivism *have* been used in a name-calling way, and this has obscured the real character and substance of philosophical debates between say empiricism and rationalism as theories of knowledge, and between positivism and realism as competing versions of the nature of social science. Althusserian Marxism has been the most recent example of such labelling games wherein empiricism is seen as a baseless pseudo-science and/or a manifestation of 'bourgeois' sociology. In this book I make it plain that I have no truck with labelling games which merely mask a typically unjustifiable assertion of the superiority of one rather crude position in what in fact turns out to be a rather more complex debate.

The acrimonious residue of this particular example of name-calling left the 'hands-on-the-data' practitioners of social research feeling that they had been unfairly vilified. This feeling was justified. Unfortunately, it led some practitioners to engage in a reverse game of name-calling, for example, labelling such terms as positivism or empiricism as 'vacuous' or 'meaningless'. This kind of reverse name-calling is by no means restricted to practicing social scientists; it has become the prerogative of academic philosophers as well, as is vividly demonstrated by Ayer or Popper who insist that those schools of thought which do not conform to their ideas of what science is, or should be, are deemed metaphysical nonsense.

These philosophers make exactly the same dangerous confusion as the practicing social scientists in so far as they obscure the respective truth claims of empiricism and rationalism under the welter of stigmatising epithets and entrenched 'resolutions' of the debate. Thus, any advance in the real substance of the debate is pre-empted by 'fixing' it on one side or the other of the stigmatising game. The dangers of this kind of obfuscation must be most apparent; the horizons of knowledge face premature and potentially permanent closure. All the arguments in this book directly challenge this name-calling game and its perpetuation by the self-appointed keepers of various closed faiths. Thus, this book attempts to address the very real issues that are obscured (and wrongly rendered 'false') by the mutual derogations involved in the game. Only in this way can knowledge of the hinterland between philosophy and the social sciences be kept moving towards an open horizon.

A corollary of the name-calling game is the over-simplification of the issues involved. This, in turn, is compounded by the rather arrogant assumption that so-called problems and issues are either already resolved, or, simply figments of the imagination of dangerous zealots and subversives (see Bulmer 1988). A clear example of this kind of thing can be seen in the context of the question of the relation between theory and evidence. It has become something of a bland sociological truism that empirical analysis is embedded in theory; a variant of the proposition that all observations are theory-laden. It is not that I would disagree with the fundamental assertion, indeed, the greater burden of the arguments of this book are concerned with teasing out some of the ramifications of this very issue. No, my worries concern those practitioners who believe that reciting the proposition something in the manner of a religious incantation is enough in itself.

For those of this persuasion it would seem that actually enunciating the credo 'empirical analysis (observation, data, and so on,) is theory-laden', somehow 'resolves' the issue and therefore absolves them from any further analysis. This sort of complacency results from an inability or unwillingness to scrutinise exactly what is meant by the term 'theory' in this context. Thus, a very narrow definition (usually of the form 'a proposition relating two or more variables, open to empirical testability or falsification'), is taken as the exclusive meaning of the term theory. This narrow definition of theory is then fed into a circuit of self-perpetuation. This is based on the premise that because empirical analysis is theory-laden, that is, we see it through the lens of either verified theoretical propositions or potentially testable ones, that therefore, as long as we know what these are (or can find out) we simply have to be aware of them in the specific inquiry in which we are engaged.

In this way only one definition of 'theory' (that is, the positivist one) is admissible to the discussion. This book attempts to go beyond these bland assertions about what theory is, or should be, and look at the way in which the term is differently employed in various theoretical schools or perspectives within sociology and social psychology, and according to different ideas about the nature of social science. With regard to these latter, there are three distinct visions of what social science is or should be, extant in social scientific practice; they are positivism, humanism and realism. The centre of interest for this book is obviously realism and thus I shall be advocating a version of it throughout. Of course, this does not mean that in so doing I shall neglect or reject everything that positivism and humanism have to offer.

By looking at different levels and types of practice in social science (that is, different methodological protocols, strategies, types of research method, theoretical schools' visions of social science and their underlying knowledge premises), I attempt to unpack the notion of 'theory' and thus deal with it in a more realistic manner. In this sense I view it as operating at a number of levels and in different types of discourse as presuppositions which govern the nature of the discourse in question. By unpacking the notion of theory in this way I attempt to address the issue of in what way or ways it is meaningful to talk of empirical inquiry as theory-laden in relation to a strictly delimited number of possibilities which are operative within the practice of social science today.

It hardly needs to be said that this involves a complex adjudication of truth claims in relation to a number of types and levels of social scientific discourse. This idea is inherently disturbing to those who believe that things should be kept simple and that the thorny problems of epistemology and ontology are *unnecessary* complications or obstacles thrown into the smoothly (and smugly) rutted path of social research. Unfortunately, this is also the way of ignorance and dogmatism, resulting in the premature closing-down of knowledge.

To those who need to cling to the security of an unquestioned methodological uniformity (Bulmer 1988, and see Appendix for further discussion), one of the most frightening aspects of what I have to say in this book is that my arguments resolutely square-up to the reality of a *limited* relativism which characterises the many-layered practices of social science. The emphasis on 'limited' is extremely important. The advocates of unquestioned uniformity confuse any other position with an unbridled, or 'anything goes' relativism; a pernicious advocation of a sociological Babel which licenses every sort of 'subversive' activity. I think that it hardly needs to be pointed out that a confusion of this order does nothing to strengthen the methodological basis of social science or to improve its standing in the wider intellectual community. Clearly there is a world of difference between the limited form of relativism that is a necessary part of my argument in this book, and an 'anything goes' Babel. Unfortunately, the clarity of this difference does not guarantee that it will be properly grasped by those who wish to keep things simple and uniform. In this sense the relativism which I espouse refers not to a desirable state of affairs but to an actual, or real one. Moreover, it is one which is a logical requirement for the postulation of the existence of rival or alternative positions to the one I prefer and advocate in this book.

A pernicious and common mistake of those advocates of the 'let us keep things simple' and 'let us keep the untidy problems of philosophy out of social science' is the unwarranted assumption that engaging in certain kinds of abstract philosophical argument automatically means that one is attacking the whole notion of empirical research. I think that most of those who read this book carefully enough will not make this mistake, but since I have been accused of this already (Bulmer 1988), I find it necessary to rebut further this quite outlandish claim.

As I said earlier, the whole point of this book is to do some preliminary work towards strengthening the methodological basis of social science. However, I also said that this cannot consist in a simple-minded rejection of abstract modes of reasoning or philosophical argument. In fact, I suggested that there is nothing inconsistent about holding both of the following views. First, the idea that there are some philosophical questions which cannot be adjudicated by appeal to empirical evidence, and second, that empirical research is an indispensable feature of social science and that *its* truth claims cannot be simply adjudicated *a priori*, for example, in the manner that Winch (1963) seems to think.

Of course, the fullness of my arguments concerning the nature of the compatibility of these two notions will follow from later detailed discussions of the relevant issues, but in the light of the accusation alluded to previously, I am afraid I need to reiterate that my position is a complex one which views both *a priori* knowledge and empirical research as complementary to each other. My argument is *against* those who hold to one of these positions *at the expense* of the other. Unfortunately, it is most commonly social scientists who hold that empirical research is privileged in this respect. Those who do hold to this view dogmatically are precisely the ones who accuse anyone who holds a different position of 'metaphysical speculation' or unnecessary obfuscations of questions which are of an indubitably empirical nature. Again, this falls back into a game of entrenched defence and attaching stigmatising labels to the 'opposition' (that is, people who hold different views).

There is nothing that I want this book to contribute more to than the dissolution of this futile exercise which can only lead to two kinds of dead-end; the unargued assertion of one position at the expense of the other, or the bland assumption that whatever problems are posed by the possibility of their complementarity are either resolved or merely superficial. In this sense 'superficiality' and its relation 'simplicity' are in the eye of the beholder, and whatever the virtues of simplicity, the desire that things should be so, must not blind us to the possibility that reality may reveal itself to be rather more complicated. To believe otherwise, that is, that simplicity rather than complexity is an intrinsic feature of reality, and of our cognitive grasp of this reality, would be naive indeed. This more than anything else is the message of this book.

1 The Possibility of Realism

INTRODUCTION

In this book I shall inquire into the prospects for, and problems of, the new realist philosophy of social science as specifically applied to sociology and social psychology. In large part, I want to argue positively and suggest that the realist project is a step in the right direction towards a more informed and sophisticated framework with which to understand social analysis and the activities of social scientists in general. Thus, in this sense I am interested in fulfilling the aims and ideals of realism by adding to the extant corpus of work on this topic. However, I also want to suggest that the realist programme is beset with problems which stand in the way of its progress towards a comprehensive and coherent alternative to the positivist or humanist programmes. Thus, in this further sense I shall adopt a highly critical but *constructive* stance towards the existing literature on realism, in an attempt to prod it towards what I consider to be a more congenial direction.

Having laid out the general approach and tenor of my argument let me now outline the more specific details as they are reflected in the sequence of the chapters. In what follows these introductory comments I shall first try to describe the distinctiveness of the realist programme as compared with its main competitors, positivism and humanism. I shall identify what I take to be the major inadequacies or weaknesses of the programme as it stands. In so doing I shall indicate the lines along which I feel realism should move in order to overcome these deficiencies. This discussion will set the terms of the basic theses of the book, centred on a critical but constructive development of the realist programme.

Thus, chapter two will begin this project by outlining the relationships between realism, epistemology and different levels of social scientific discourse. In this respect I believe that realism has so far neglected to analyse or generally come to terms with the very different roles and functions that social scientific discourses perform. As a consequence realism has been unable satisfactorily to apprehend the manifold connections between epistemological premises and

7

theoretical and methodological discourses within sociology and social psychology. I outline a framework for the analysis of these elements, and trace out its implications for the realist programme.

Chapter 3 then connects these implications to the problem of the validity of realist claims. I argue that realists are either ambiguous on this issue or, propose validity claims such as 'practical adequacy' which are themselves insufficient. I also question the realist strategy of according a privileged role to ontological factors in the construction of knowledge and truth claims. I think this strategy is misguided for a number of reasons, but mainly because it has the net effect of artificially narrowing down knowledge claims and unnecessarily restricting innovative developments in social science.

In chapter 4 I relate the arguments advanced in chapters 2 and 3 to the problem of the relation of theory and method. In so doing I attempt to develop some ideas on social ontology as well as raise the issue of the status of causal claims in social science in general, and realism in particular. Thus, I attempt to indicate the importance of what I call the 'implicate order' of social science and sketch in some of its contours. As a consequence this leads me to advance an argument for the importance of including acausal phenomena within realism's possible objects of inquiry.

Chapter 5 continues to engage with ontological concerns, this time with a more focussed examination of the nature of social ontology. Basically, my argument is that although realists advance a notion of social ontology as stratified, I feel their model is not stratified enough. That is, it does not include certain qualitatively distinct features of social reality, which possess powers and produce effects within the social realm. Thus, my argument is designed to extend the possible range of social objects for realism.

In the following chapter I scrutinise the implications of all these arguments for the way in which realists understand the nature of, and relationship between, social scientific language and 'lay' or everyday language. In this context I develop an argument which opposes the notion that there is an easy continuity and interchange between the two. Here I question Giddens' (1976, 1979, 1984, 1986) influential notion of 'slippage' between lay and scientific terms and suggest that whilst in *some* instances there may be some degree of slippage, his notion can definitely not be applied 'across the board'. I argue that there are fundamental differences in kind between certain technical social scientific terms and those of everyday life and that in many of these cases, slippage does not occur. In those cases where it does occur the slippage has to be understood in a highly qualified way and thus the universality of Giddens' claims must be rejected.

Throughout the book, but particularly in the penultimate chapter I deliberate on the prospects of realism as they bear upon two related and important questions in social science. First is the rather formal question of the nature of the relationship between theory and evidence in social analysis. This question feeds directly into the other; what is the relationship between the realist image of social science and the practicalities of social research? My claims here would be that the position or positions which I have developed in the book enable responses to these two questions which are broader in scope and explanatory range than those that would follow from the realist programme as it presently stands.

THE DISTINCTIVENESS OF THE REALIST PROJECT

The relatively recent proliferation of work applying realist ideas to the domain of social science (Harre and Secord 1972, Harré 1979, Keat 1971, Keat and Urry 1975, Bhaskar 1979, Benton 1981, Manicas and Secord 1983, Sayer 1984) has to be understood as a response to the traditional or standard 'positivist' view of the nature of science and scientific activity. In this respect realism in social science is an attempt to provide an alternative account of the scientific nature of the enterprise of social analysis to that provided by positivism. Thus, realism insists that the natural science model is a valid exemplar, but that positivism has mischaracterised and misrepresented the form and operation of this exemplar.

This focus of interest distinguishes realism from the alternative to positivist social science, humanism. Humanism by contrast, rejected the whole notion of the credibility of the natural science paradigm as an examplar for social analysis. For the humanist the subject matter of the social sciences (conscious intentional human beings) was so radically discrepant from that of the natural sciences (inanimate material objects) that it required a quite distinct approach. Now whilst realism attempts to embrace the humanist characterisation of the differences in subject matter of the natural and social sciences it does not, thereby, require us to reject many of the original features of the natural science examplar. As I have said, what it does require is to reject the specific *positivist* version of this examplar. Therefore, in what follows I shall briefly outline the major characteristics of the positivist view of social scientific activity.

THE POSITIVIST ORTHODOXY

Positivism holds the view that the scientific study of society, in method and procedure, should resemble as closely as possible the scientific study of natural phenomena, for instance, as in mechanics (Harré and Secord 1972). Thus, the study of sociology (and social psychology) could proceed as if the objects of their study presented no special problems for analysis. The aim in the positivist vision was to produce general laws of social behaviour (like the general laws of natural phenomena) which could be built up and verified (or falsified) through factual observations and the construction of appropriate experiments or test procedures.

Thus behaviourism and many experimental schools in social psychology, and functionalism (Merton 1968) in sociology attempted to gain predictive and explanatory knowledge of the external social world by identifying the 'variables' which produce social behaviour. On this view, scientific knowledge is generated in a painstaking cumulative manner through controlled observation, thus ensuring that the results will not be speculative or hypothetical, but grounded in empirical reality. The general role of theory is thus to provide a logical organisation or conceptual depiction of the regular relationships that are observed to exist in the social world.

The positivist idea that these regular relationships also express *causal* relationships is derived from the Humean notion of causality which stresses that whenever there exist regular conjunctions of events (a regular sequence in which one event follows another), then this also expresses a causal relationship, such that when it is found through observation and experience that event B always follows event A, then A is said to cause B. Now although in this conception theory is, as it were, subordinated to an organisational role this has not always been linked in positivism with a naively empiricist view.

In sociology, for example, Merton (1968) has taken pains to avoid the narrow-mindedness of the naive empiricist view that empirical research can proceed, as it were, 'blind'. Thus, in Merton's view empirical generalisations may be a necessary prerequisite for the establishment of theories, but they are not to be confused with systematic theory itself. Systematic theory consists of sets of logically

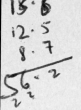

)ositions from which can be deduced empirically
)es.

rton's position does not break completely with
empiricism; in fact it represents a sophisticated version of empiricism.
This is because although Merton pays lip-service to the difference
between 'empirical generalisations' and theory, the validity of the
latter is finally arbitrated in terms of test procedures which are non-
theoretical, namely measurement against the observed 'objective'
empirical world. (The same is true of Popper 1959; see chapter 3).
Thus if theories are tested by non-theoretical criteria, their acceptance as corroborated (validated) theories must be a result of their
concordance with (and thus logical organisation of) the empirical
world.

A central feature of this formulation is the radical denial of rationalist epistemology in any form whatsoever. For positivism any autonomous role for rational connections of theoretical concepts in the
final determination of what counts as valid (corroborated, falsifiable)
knowledge must be rejected. To do otherwise would be to admit to
the status of scientific knowledge just those sorts of statements which
are anathema to empirical science, and which positivism seeks to
exclude. The notion of the rational determination of knowledge
amounts to the endorsement of meaningless metaphysical specu-
lations (Ayer 1971).

Keat and Urry (1975) have pointed out that the positivist view of
theory renders problematic the status of theoretical terms, which are
sometimes a feature of theories and laws of social life. Very often
such theoretical terms refer to entities or events which cannot be
perceived or directly observed, for example, electrical or magnetic
fields in physical science, or anomie or alienation in social science.
The problem arises because the 'scientificity' of a term, or statement
containing the term, is compromised if it is not possible to decide
upon its truth or falsity by direct empirical and observational means.

The positivist resolution of this problem is typically made by distinguishing between a theoretical (or non-observational) language, and
an observational (or non-theoretical) language. The connection
between these two languages is made by correspondence rules via
which the definitions of theoretical terms can be given to them by
means of statements containing only observational terms. Thus, the
scientificity of statements about the social (or natural) world is
'ensured', if theoretical statements contain no non-observational
terms at all. Alternatively, if they do, they must be ultimately

translatable via correspondence rules into observational terms. In social theory, the problem of the correspondence between theoretical and observational terms is reflected in the concern with the 'operationalisation' of concepts and rendering them empirically 'testable'.

The notion of a correspondence between theoretical and observational terms in positivism effectively narrows the meaning and role of theory to the expression of observed regularities, and thus moves quite away from a concern with the rational connections between concepts in the development of scientific knowledge. In this sense positivist knowledge and theory always remains constrained by empiricist limitations. These then, are the basic contours of the positivist position that realism intends to replace.

However, as I indicated before, realism also wants to reject the radical anti-naturalist stand espoused by humanism whilst attempting to preserve some of its more valuable insights. Thus, whilst humanism rejects general laws and causal explanation in social life (see Winch 1963 and Louch 1966) realism would wish to retain these modes of explanation albeit in a completely reworked form. Similarly, although realists would find room for *verstehen* (interpretive understanding) modes of explanation most would reject the claim that such explanations are exhaustive. The general relationship between realism and humanism is complicated, entailing many relations of dependence on and independence from each other and these will become more apparent as the discussion unfolds. Therefore, let me now attempt to delineate the realist position in brief outline.

THE REALIST ALTERNATIVE

Realists aim to resuscitate and reincorporate some of the concerns of natural science into a social science shorn of its positivistic assumptions. Harré and Secord (1972), Keat and Urry (1975) and Bhaskar (1979) have all attempted to vindicate a philosophy of social science along these lines. As these authors represent it, the realist version of naturalism differs from the positivist version in two principal ways.

Firstly, for realists, the Humean notion of causality as expressed in the idea of observable, regular conjunctions of events, is not an adequate conception of causality, since in essence it reduces to what amounts to a description and/or prediction of observed and observable phenomena rather than a true explanation of them. For the realist a true explanation must go beyond the establishment of observed empirical regularities and posit causal or generative mechanisms which underlie these regularities (conjunctions of events) and actually produce them. Thus for the realist, to say that B was caused by A on the basis of an observed regularity between the two is a misapplication of the concept of causality. A real causal explanation must answer the question of why these regularities exist in terms of the underlying mechanisms which generate them. Since such causal mechanisms, as it were, underlie and produce observable regularities as *effects* of their operation, the possibility arises of these mechanisms being unobserved.

Thus, in the realist scheme of things there is a realm of 'theoretical' entities whose meaning for the analyst cannot be simply given in terms of observations. Now whilst such theoretical entities may be unobservable, they are no less *real* than observable ones and thus 'theory' for the realist becomes a means of describing the relations between the unobservable causal mechanisms (or structures) and their effects in social life. This has an apparent advantage over positivism in that knowledge in realism does not have to be construed as a simple conceptual appropriation of the observed or experienced world; that is, that theoretical and substantive knowledge is limited by what we can glean through our senses. Thus, seemingly the positing of the existence of theoretical entities also decrees that the realm of theory be broadened out beyond the given sensorily apprehended world.

In the realist scheme of things the positivist focus on empirical regularities and rigid deductive nomological forms of proof and argument has been superseded by the realist search for causal generative mechanisms which underlie the surface or observational manifestation of constant conjunctions. As a result, the ontological priority accorded by positivists to observation languages and experience in the determination of the meaning and testing of scientific statements (that is, the verificationist theory of meaning) is, for the realist, displaced by a concern with unobservable (or relatively unobservable) theoretical entities, the meaning of whose concepts can be understood 'independently of the construction of test procedures which enable us to verify indirectly the presence or absence of the items referred to by these terms' (Keat and Urry 1975, p. 39). Thus also, for Harré and Secord (1972, p. 73) 'the key to the understanding of the epistemology and logic of creative science and thus to understanding its basic methodology is to be found in the notion of a *model'*. In this way models which represent real things or processes (and which are like their subjects in some ways and unlike them in others) stand for the causal mechanisms which produce or generate the non-random pattern that has been observed.

In rejecting the Humean notion of causality and lawfulness, the realists wish to replace it with a notion of scientific laws as applying to 'the causal properties of structures that exist and operate in the world' rather than to 'events or classes of events, regularly or stochastically conjoined' (Manicas and Secord 1983, p. 402). Bhaskar (1979) argues that the empirical regularities with which positivists concern themselves are really only relevant to experimental type situations where there is a closed system produced by a high degree of control over the number of real mechanisms at work. The deductive nomological model of explanation presupposes an ontology of events and closed systems, but the rare characteristic of closure found in laboratory situations is then illicitly assumed to be a general characteristic of the world outside the laboratory. Bhaskar therefore argues that the D-N model is inapplicable in situations not consisting of events in a closed system. That is, the D-N model is inappropriate to the real world outside of the laboratory since the latter is an *open* system.

It follows on from this that in this sense realism breaks with the positivist idea that explanation and prediction are symmetrical. Instead, attention is focussed on isolating and describing the real causal mechanisms at work in producing the world of events and on 'reconstructively explaining past events in terms of the conjunctional operation of particular mechanisms' (Pateman 1987, p. 8). As Manicas and Secord have put it;

> we may often be in a position to explain some event once it has occurred, when it would have been impossible – even in principle – to predict it. Although the relatively enduring structures of the world have definite (and knowable) causal properties, it is only under closure that explanation and prediction are symmetrical. In an open world, the configurations of structures and structural processes are not predictable. Indeed, for the standard view of science, the world is a determined concatenation of contingent events; for the realist it it a contingent concatenation of real structures. And this difference is monumental. The past is, in a sense, 'determined'. That is, what happened can be causally *explained*. But the future is not determined precisely because the complexly

related structures and systems of the world are constantly being reconfigured [in contingent ways]. (1983, p. 403)

Just as realism does not concern itself with prediction, since this is only applicable under situations of closure, so also the criticism of falsification has no place in realism since 'decisive falsification of claims is always going to be extremely difficult where laboratory experiments (experimental closures) are not practically or alternatively feasible' (Pateman 1987, p. 9).

Realism views both the world and science (and hence social science) as stratified; different sciences focus on different aspects of the world. Thus, 'the social sciences focus on the structures produced by human agency, studying how these relate to each other and to enduring practices' whilst 'social psychological science focuses on individuals in their interaction with one another and with social institutions and how this activity relates to the larger social structures' (Manicas and Secord 1983, p. 408). Similarly, within sociology itself Bhaskar distinguishes between human agency and social structures as quite different aspects of social reality.

More generally realists have argued that the positivist stress on the unity of the natural and social sciences led them to undervalue an important differentiating feature of the natural and social sciences; their respective concerns with non-human and human objects of inquiry. Thus, for the realist, the humanist point that humans (unlike the inanimate objects of natural science) are conscious intentional beings able to respond to, and act back upon, external forces that affect their behaviour, must be incorporated into the framework of social science. The attempt to do this has resulted in the establishment of somewhat different problems and emphases in the work of the realists. Firstly, Harré and Secord (1972) and Harré (1979) have attempted to apply a realist framework to the discipline of social psychology. This they have done by replacing the positivistic assumptions of traditional experimental (psychological) social psychology, particularly the mechanistic conception of the social actor and (his/her) action which is a legacy of the application of the Humean notion of causality to the study of social behaviour.

The displacement of an outmoded notion of causality whereby the actor is viewed simply as the *transmitter* of the external demands of the causal variables (stimuli), goes hand in hand with the recognition that (unlike the inanimate objects of the natural sciences), the human being should be viewed as a spontaneous locus of causality. That is, the human being should be conceived of as a *generator* of social behaviour instead of simply as a transmitter of external constraints. For Harré and Secord the main causal mechanism involved in the generation of social behaviour is 'self-direction according to the meaning ascribed (by the actor) to the situation'. Thus 'reason-explanations' became an important focus in this form of realism.

Keat and Urry also believe that the value of 'reason-explanations' or 'reasons as causes' must be admitted as a species of explanation although they are more cautious than Harré (1979) in suggesting that they see no reason to limit sociology to this level of analysis. Bhaskar, however, is less restrained. He claims that his 'causal theory of the mind' is a necessary prerequisite for the understanding of 'any theoretical or practical activity' (1979, p. 205). Since he also claims that social structures (which constitute the basic objects of social analysis) 'do not exist independently of the activities they govern' (p. 48) then the explication of social structure *ipso facto* involves invocation of reason explanations. However, for Bhaskar the advocacy of such explanations must not be confused with the hermeneuticist belief that actors accounts (beliefs, perceptions) are incorrigible.

I shall have something more to say about the issue of the causal status of reason explanations (as well as the other issues covered here) later in the discussion. However, what I have said thus far about realism as an alternative to positivism represents a general, albeit brief, summary of its basic parameters. In these broad and general terms, realism presents a formidable challenge to the standard positivist orthodoxy. As I stated in my introduction, it is in the light of the recognition of the promise of this already substantial body of work that I wish to enter into a constructive critique of, and dialogue with, this corpus of work. Thus, I shall now turn to a discussion and delineation of what I take to be some of the deficiencies of the realist project.

DEFICIENCIES IN THE REALIST PROGRAMME

(1) Summarising the realist programme it becomes apparent that many epistemological questions have not been systematically worked through by realist writers. Associated with this is the lack of a systematic understanding or characterisation of the stratification of social scientific discourses. This is surprising since the realists make much of the notion of the stratification of science and the world in

a formal sense. But that is the point; they rest content with statements of the formal principle but they do not follow through their ramifications. Were they to do so they would find that even *within* specific disciplines, such as sociology and psychology, there are distinct *levels* and *types* of discourses which perform different roles and functions in relation to each other and which are complexly interwoven.

As a by-product of this lack of attention by realists to these phenomena, they are also often content to operate with an undifferentiated notion of theory. What a stratified view of discourses does is draw attention to the multi-levelled nature of theory and theoretical presuppositions as they relate to different aspects of social scientific discourses. In chapter 2 I want to argue that basic questions of epistemology and ontology ramify through these different theoretical levels and produce different effects not only within the theoretical levels but also within the methodological, practical and strategic discourses of social research. It is this question of the way in which basic knowledge premises push through into the structure of social research practices at different levels of theoretical presuppositions and ontological imagery that is the specific focus of my interest in chapter 2.

Particularly important here, is the question of the linguistic forms in terms of which different levels and types of discourse are represented. Basic questions of perception and cognition are tied up with these forms of expression and mediate the meaningful content of the discourses. It is precisely this sort of emphasis that is absent from realist writing. Much is indicated or implied in a nominal way about 'theory', knowledge, ontology and so on, but there is little in the way of systematic theorising about them. Now one of the reasons for this absence in realist writing might be that such a primarily 'analytic' frame of reference may, on the face of it, appear to sanction an idealist mode of analysis, and this is at odds with the realists materialistic predilections with *real* causal mechanisms and generative structures.

However, idealism could not be further from my thoughts in proposing this framework. Indeed, the primarily epistemological framework which I present is designed ultimately to sanction or underwrite an objectivist epistemology (which includes knowledge of both material and ideal objects) and an objectivist ontology (which posits the objective/real existence of material and ideal entities). This is a necessary part of my project since I feel that many realists have prematurely rejected certain forms of objectivism on the grounds that it is inherently allied to positivism. (For the most unqualified rejection of objectivism from someone sympathetic to the realist position, see Giddens 1984.)

The deleterious consequences of the premature and sometimes wholesale rejection of objectivism is just one of the many problematic areas that are opened up for a realism which does not attend to the systematic analysis of the stratified discourses of social science. As the issue of objectivism highlights, these problems appear to be of an epistemological and/or ontological nature.

(2) The first specific epistemological deficiency within the realist scheme of things, I would argue, is an inability to come to terms with, or meet the full force of the critique of empiricism in social science despite realists attempts to do so, or claims to have done so. This has even led one realist writer to shy away completely from the term 'empiricism' on the grounds that it has become 'devalued' or 'purely pejorative' (Sayer 1984, p. 14). This is an extreme example of avoidance, but inattention to the full implications and the many different modes of empiricism within sociology and social psychology is perhaps the more usual tendency. Unfortunately, the characteristic stance on empiricism by realists is the assumption that the empiricist limitations on knowledge imposed by positivism have been transcended.

Indeed, most realists assert with confidence that realism breaks with the foundationist epistemology of positivism which decrees that the test of truth of propositions is 'correspondence' between theory and data and thus that hypotheses are to be tested against the 'facts'. For the realist there are no transhistorical, theory-neutral data; instead, knowledge is viewed as a social and historical product. As Manicas and Secord put it 'there is no preinterpreted "given" and the test of truth therefore cannot be correspondence' (1983), p. 401). However, science aims at inventing theories which (in some sense) represent the world. Accordingly, the sciences develop their own *rational* criteria in terms of which theory is accepted or rejected. Manicas and Secord point out that these criteria are rational

> because on realist terms, there is a world that exists independently of our cognizing experience. Since our theories are constitutive of the known world but *not* of the *world*, we may always be wrong, but *not* anything goes. (p. 401)

Now while the declared break with foundationism and the notion of correspondence is definitely an intentional move away from empiricism, again, these programmatic statements do not go far enough in seeking out the multi-faceted ramifications of empiricism. It may be true that the various social sciences develop their own 'rational' criteria for the evaluation of theories. But such a characterisation does not do justice to the variegated validity criteria that exist within specific social science disciplines, such as sociology and social psychology. Different validity criteria exist for a number of reasons but perhaps the most visible of these is the fact that these disciplines are not unitary but composed of different, sometimes overlapping, discourses (frameworks, approaches, schools) which relate to each other in terms of varying degrees of explanatory competitiveness.

In this sense the nature of a unitary set of 'rational' criteria for sociology breaks down into a (limited) number of 'rationalities' some sharing part of this content with others, others not. I shall develop this line of argument in more detail in the next chapter, but here I simply want to draw attention to the fact that this differentiation within social scientific disciplines is, to use realist phraseology, a fact that 'exists independently of our knowledge' and therefore, must play a role in our understanding of these sciences. Apart from the breakdown of a unitary basis it is also clear that many discourses or schools of social science *already* have connections with empiricist modes of generating and evaluating knowledge (for instance, symbolic interactionism, ethnomethodology, middle-range theorising, and so on).

Given this situation, it is of paramount importance to understand that a realist appropriation of social science as it *already stands* will not be a simple affair of changing our conception of the methodology or rationality of these disciplines. To say that correspondence no longer applies and that social science is about inventing representative theories about the world misses out the fact that specific forms of theorising take place in the context of *already established theoretical* presuppositions, for example, about the efficacy of middle-range theorising or the importance of indexical accounts.

Since realism in itself has no substantive theoretical content but is, in a sense, a meta-theory of methodology, in a non-pejorative sense it must always 'attach' itself to established social sciences or schools of theory. Now unless realism comes to terms with the already established character of these disciplines and theories, that is, unless it understands the ineradicable connections with empiricism that *are constitutive* of some of these discourses, then realism is likely to import them uncritically into the realist domain. Thus, changing the rules (of correspondence, or of the nature of scientific activity) at the meta-methodological level is not enough; the empiricist basis of much social science will remain undisturbed unless empiricism is tackled at root in the constitutive domains of social science.

In chapter 3 I shall develop this argument further and take up the question of the way empiricism in fact has been unwittingly imported by realists. In this respect there are three areas which are of paramount importance. First, realists have appropriated large areas of the humanist project but in my view have failed to eradicate the empiricist epistemological underpinnings which form its base. Sometimes, in such instances it seems that while realists are content to condemn positivist empiricism out of hand, they are unwilling to reject humanist empiricism which, while possessing a different form (Layder 1982), nonetheless has an identical origin and structure as a theory of knowledge.

Second, for related and other reasons, realist validity claims are often grounded in unacknowledged empiricist premises. Now it is the 'unacknowledged' nature of these premises which are of importance here. I am not arguing that there should be a blanket dismissal of empiricist claims or 'domains' of knowledge. In fact, contra the current realist trend, I will argue that realist knowledge premises must coexist with other already established epistemological positions such as empiricism, although the nature of this coexistence has to be carefully worked out. In this sense there can be no 'wishing away' of empiricist (or indeed, rationalist) knowledge claims, but the actual effects of empiricism for particular validity claims must be carefully mapped out, and thus, openly acknowledged. It is the realist assumption that the problem of empiricist effects has been swept aside in the wake of the new realist theory of knowledge (no matter how ambiguous or vague this turns out to be under rigorous scrutiny), that prevents just this kind of mapping and acknowledgement.

The final area of empiricist 'importation' is related to the other two, but concerns specifically the question of ontology. Realists are extremely fond of emphasising the importance of ontological features as undergirding the real causal structures and generative mechanisms that are the objects of science. However, often specific ontological features are proposed by realists (for instance, Bhaskar or Giddens) and presented as part of a transcendental analysis with the effect that they are conceived of as irreducible and fundamental ontological elements. However, this is often accomplished by strategic or definitional fiat rather than by the persuasion of authoritative and informed reason. The net result is that ontological features in general are often 'privileged' in an analogous way to that of brute fact and empirical data in the positivist vision of science. Again, this becomes another way in which empiricist elements are imported into realist arguments and produce effects which are unacknowledged.

(3) The argument about empiricism runs into a more general point about epistemology in the realist scheme of things. In this sense, the realist assault on the foundationist epistemology of positivism is a rather cavalier affair which is not sufficiently sensitive to the complexity of the issues. After all, the question of empiricism is not an isolatable question; it only really makes sense in the context of the debate between itself and the other major and opposed theory of knowledge – rationalism. However, realists are prone to silence on the question of rationalism. How are we to interpret this relative silence?

We could read the realist position as a tacit endorsement of rationalism. As Manicas and Secord say, each science develops its own 'rational' criteria in terms of which theories are accepted or rejected. However, one searches in vain for any systematic exposition of the influence of rationalism in its technical sense as relating to *a priori* forms and bases of knowledge. Thus, whilst sciences could be said to develop their own 'rational' criteria, in this form this might mean nothing more than that the criteria are the result of reasoned forms of argument, and while the technical use of the term rationalism certainly does not preclude this meaning, here is a definite sense in which it goes beyond simply licensing the operation of reason.

It is in relation to the underdeveloped characterisation of the issues germane to the epistemological debate between empiricism and rationalism that I develop in chapter 3 an extension of the analysis in chapter 2, and which attempts to map the criss-crossing of the effects of both empiricist and rationalist knowledge premises on social scientific knowledge. In particular here, I attempt to develop further the theme begun in chapter 2, that the rational or network properties of theoretical discourses have a role to play in the fashioning of the objects of social scientific analysis.

(4) The next area of concern in relation to the realist project is not so much to do with an ambiguity or insufficiency in the arguments or concerns of the extant realist 'package' of ideas; rather, it has to do with an absence. The absence centres on two connected issues;

the general model of social ontology and the treatment of causality implicit in the realist project.

Although realists have been ruthlessly efficient in rooting out the superficiality of the positivist notion of causality as constant conjunctions of events, and equally proficient in formulating an alternative based on the causal powers of generative structures and mechanisms, they have, nonetheless, concurred with positivism over the overriding importance of causal phenomena in general. That is, whilst disagreeing about the way in which causal phenomena may be characterised, realists have agreed that the most important feature of social scientific activity is the search for causal phenomena and tracing their causal effects.

I want to argue that realism should break away from this overriding concern with causality since it restricts both the explanatory power and the explanatory content of realism. I hasten to add, of course, that this is *not* a call for the complete abandonment of causal concerns; far from it. What I am arguing is that realist explanation should not be *limited* to causal explanation. Thus, I believe its explanatory base should be expanded to include forms of *acausal phenomena* where these are informative about that section of the social world under scrutiny. Characterised in a slightly different way I want to suggest that realism includes within its explanatory scope an ontologically different order of phenomena from that defined in and through the problematic of causality.

As I say, this would not be to jettison causality completely, but would be merely to reinforce the realist injunction to view the world as stratified in the first place. Thus causal concerns and acausal concerns would represent different *levels* of explanation as well as different *levels* of social reality. However, I want to argue more than this and suggest that beyond the representation of two ontological domains, the causal and the acausal, the two orders are related and that this relationship, of necessity, must be expressed *acausally*.

In chapter 4 I attempt to flesh out such a model in the form of what I term the explicate (causal) and the implicate (acausal) orders of social reality. In this respect I specifically focus on the acausal interdependencies of the two orders as they are represented in the realms of *practice* and *ideas*. Thus, I examine ideas and practice in relation to questions of theory and method in sociology. My general argument is that incorporation of the implicate order *adds to* any substantive or theoretical account of the relationship between theory and method.

(5) Another aspect of the question of the stratification of social reality concerns the nature of (macro) social structure. Stated briefly and directly, I feel that realists in general have been unable to sustain a notion of macro structure as possessing properties which can be understood to be *relatively* independent of the agents whose behaviour is subject to their influence. Realists fall into two camps on this. There are those, such as Harré (1979, 1981), who dismiss the idea of macro structures as merely rhetorical devices which appear in agents accounts but have no existential or real status beyond these accounts. In its simplest terms this seems to be a gross form of reductionism which is quite contrary to the notions of stratification of science and reality which are at the centrepoint of much realist writing.

Thankfully, other realist social psychologists do not seem to share Harré's view (see comments by Manicas and Secord 1983, p. 408–9) because such a position *ipso facto* seems to preclude any sensible or disciplined dialogue between 'realist' social psychology and the macro-structural analyses which represent perhaps the dominant mode in sociology. However, the other camp in realism, perhaps the more sociologically oriented, whilst endorsing an ontological distinction between people and social structures (Bhaskar 1979, Keat and Urry 1975, Giddens 1984) are at best ambiguous on the relative independence issue.

These latter writers put forward a view of structure which seems to undercut the notion of relative independence. Let it be clear that I am *not* arguing for a reified view of social structure such that structure has some essential and operationally independent life of its own which is completely beyond the control of human beings. To argue for a relative independence is simply to argue that macro structures have properties which enable them to constrain as well as facilitate human action from 'outside' *as well* as from within. Constraints and facilities do not *simply* exist in the minds of human actors, they are most crucially, socially generated and socially located resources which are drawn into agents' activities from external cultural 'funds'.

Bhaskar in particular insists on the concept-dependence of social structures which in my view severely compromises the possibility of an objectivist conception of macro-structure as I have outlined it above. Giddens more clearly sides with a radical anti-objectivist stance whilst holding to the view that macro-structures are not simple aggregations of (and thus reducible to) micro situations (as in Harré,

1981, Collins 1981, Knorr-Cetina 1981). Whilst agreeing wholeheartedly with these latter sentiments I feel that Giddens' attempt to equate objectivism with positivism (and naturalism) is misguided and only serves to narrow down the explanatory domain of sociological and/or social realist analysis (see Layder 1981, 1982, 1987).

Again, to be absolutely clear, I am using the term objectivism in the sense which endorses the notion of a social reality independent of our 'cognising experience' but which nonetheless is one of the primary objects of social analysis. In this sense objectivism seems totally consonant with the realist project. Objectivism here, is *not* meant to convey the positivist sense in which knowledge objectively corresponds to reality, and/or that such knowledge is thus value-neutral. None of these senses are entailed in the objectivism I refer to above. As I say, the way I use it seems concordant with realist ideas; thus I am surprised by the premature rejection of it by many realist writers.

(6) In another area I think the realists have ceded too much to hermeneutics or interpretive sociology in their effort to embrace humanistic insights. In a sense this is the converse of the tendency to undervalue objectivism. In this respect I believe wholeheartedly that actors' accounts and reasons must not be discounted or rejected and that they must serve, in some sense, as *a species* of explanation in the social sciences. However, to elevate reason explanations to the state of the only, or the most important, form of explanation is mistaken.

It is feasible to understand actors' reasons as 'causal' in the existential sense that human agents are in the final analysis responsible for producing their own behaviour. That is, in the face of whatever external constraint or coercion, it is the person him or herself who must embody the enacted response (Sartre 1966). *In this sense*, and this sense only, a person's account of, or stated reasons for, the action may be said to have possessed causal power in producing the behavioural response. Of course, this is not to deny that other, 'external' factors, such as the degree and type of constraint or coercion, would not have entered into the actor's deliberations before acting. It is merely to say that in some part – and the exact amount would be an empirical matter – the persons' reasons may have been causally influential.

In this quite circumscribed sense reason explanations may be thought of as a species of causal explanation. However, beyond this, reason explanations have limited value. To imply anything else is to court the whole problem of reductionism and methodological individualism from which most realists wish to escape. This is where someone like Bhaskar tries to move in several opposing directions at the same time. Having rejected methodological individualism, Bhaskar then goes on to underscore the centrality of reason explanations as causal (1979), but, we may ask, causal for what? As I have said, beyond the subjective moment of a person's pre-action deliberations, the notion of reason as cause cannot begin to explain the institutional context of action in anything other than a reductionist way.

I shall say more about this later in the book, although it is worth noting here that Bhaskar leaves this inadequate explanatory alternative wide open through his notion of the concept-dependence of social structures. Thus, because social structures are said to be concept-dependent (and possess no relative autonomy) they are always implicated (instanciated) in the constitutive doings of idea- (or concept-) bearing social beings. In this case an unbroken ontological continuity is fashioned between people and social structures – quite contrary to Bhaskar's insistence that they are different. In the same sense Giddens ties the existence of social structure to its instanciations in situated activity and thus affirms the same ontological dissolution. And, although Bhaskar and Giddens may not wish to associate themselves with Harré's realism, the contradictions and tensions in their conceptual apparatuses constantly push them in this direction.

Similarly, although Winch's (1963) attack on social scientific naturalism may not suit the realist belief in the possibility of naturalism, nonetheless, his notion of the 'elucidation of frames of meaning' as the central task of social study is much closer to (although, admittedly not identical with) many realist formulations of the role of reason explanations than they would want to admit. The similarities are even more striking when it comes to understanding the relationship between the language of social study and the language of everyday life. Here Giddens and Winch in particular share the view that there is constant interchange between two systems of language and they constantly influence each other. Again, I believe this has to do with the mistaken *elevation* of the role and importance of actors' accounts and reason explanations in social analysis. It is important to have a realistic (in the pragmatic sense) appreciation of the role of reasons, accounts and lay terms in social science without either over-valuing or underplaying their importance.

(7) Typically, realists have been quite reserved about the pragmatic

features of the realist project. In particular, the nature of the theory-evidence link in social science and the implications of this for the actual practice of social research has tended to take a back seat. This, of course, is related to the question of the validity claims of realism and the sorts of epistemological issues that I have discussed already. However, the importance of the formal question of the nature of the theory-evidence link needs to be underscored since this connects most crucially with the question of the practicalities of social research, and this, after all, must be the *raison d'être* of any 'science' which intends to be empirically engaged.

In particular, realism needs to tackle the major question of how its meta-methodological insights can be made to subserve either established or innovative strategies of social research. So far realism has offered more in the way of proscriptions rather than prescriptions. This has the rather unfortunate effect of narrowing down options and closing down potential lines of communication between different traditions and schools of theory. Much of what I say in this book is intended to produce the opposite effect. That is, my arguments are intended to open up the potential scope (and hence power) of realist-influenced explanations in social science. It is also intended to establish lines of communication and dialogue with other traditions and schools. Of course, I realise that all forms of social action, including writing, often produce unintended effects.

2 Epistemology and Levels of Discourse

In this chapter I begin the task of developing a framework with which to understand the relationship between different levels of discourse and activity within the social sciences of sociology and social psychology. Ultimately, my purpose is to place realism within the stratified discursive elements of social science. Realism must be able to situate itself in this stratified context in order that its interventions and prescriptions will be firmly anchored in the complex interweavings of epistemological, ontological, theoretical and methodological practices of social science as it is presently constituted. It is in relation to this framework that I shall later assess the validity claims of realism. In what follows I begin by indicating the importance of the epistemological debate between empiricism and rationalism, but I will reserve a more detailed discussion of these issues until chapter 3. After outlining the contours of this debate I will define what I mean by 'discourse' and 'levels of discourse', before going on to sketch out other discursive levels that are of importance in situating realism in relation to other discourses.

EPISTEMOLOGY AND CONCEPTIONS OF SOCIAL SCIENCE

Realism has largely been silent on the most influential debate within philosophy about the nature and modes of acquisition of knowledge which has been the debate between rationalism and empiricism. The advantages and disadvantages of each of these approaches to knowledge were disputed with some ferocity by the proponents of each especially in the 17th and 18th centuries. The major figures in the debate were Descartes in the 17th century for the rationalists and Hume in the 18th century for empiricism, whilst Kant (also in the 18th century) had great sympathy with the basic premises of the rationalist argument. The 20th century, however, has seen empiricism very much in the ascendency, with figures like Russell and those of the logical empiricist school like Frege, Carnap and Ayer.

Empiricism insists that knowledge is acquired directly through

27

experience and perception, and that no substantial body of knowledge about the world can be attained independently of experience
and sense perception. Rationalists on the other hand, have stressed
the role of the intellect or reason in the acquisition of knowledge
and have attempted to show that it is possible to obtain knowledge
a priori, or independently of the experienced world. However, there
are many variants of empiricism and rationalism reflected in the work
of different authors. In chapter 3 it will be necessary to be much
more specific about these issues, whilst here I want to restrict myself
to some general statements.

I take the debate between rationalism and empiricism to be central
not only to epistemological arguments within philosophy itself, but
also to the question of the nature of social science. In suggesting
this I am opposing orthodoxies which either favour some form of
empiricism, or (as in realism), whilst apparently critical of empiricism, do not fully engage with the problems posed by rationalist
arguments (see chapter 3). Another orthodoxy, especially in sociology and social psychology is to ignore or dismiss the relevance of
the debate on the (erroneous) grounds that it has been transcended
or resolved in some way (Elias 1978). Yet others ignore the debate
on the grounds that it appears to yield negligible consequences for
the brute and very practical processes of research. It should be
apparent already that I disagree wholeheartedly with the assumptions
on which these orthodoxies are based.

However, more importantly, realism has prematurely abandoned
the debate between empiricism and rationalism and its ramifications,
and has done so for two main reasons. The first is by assuming that
realism has resolved the debate in some way, and that under its
auspices social science will no longer be plagued by empiricist restrictions. However, I argue that much realist work is implicitly influenced by residual attachments to empiricism. The second reason is
that realism pays insufficient attention to rationalist principles (in the
particular way in which I define them) and thus implicitly limits
the scope, richness and potential of theoretical discourse and the
possibilities of theoretical advance.

Although the present discussion relies on drawing a contrast
between empiricism and rationalism, it does not mean that specific
authors can be neatly compartmentalised under these labels. Cottingham (1984) makes this point, and I would like to endorse his
views with respect to the present work. I would also like to extend
the argument to cover all the 'isms' discussed here; they must be

regarded as 'cluster concepts' or concepts which denote a cluster of features.

Just as there are various strands or variants of rationalism and empiricism so, too, there are clusters of features associated with the terms positivism, humanism and realism. Even what I shall in the next section identify as 'theoretical discourses' do not denote homogeneous and exact doctrines. There are many criss-crossing strands in all these traditions of thought, and the emphasis will vary from author to author. An adjunct of this is that there are often areas of overlap between the traditions of thought and that therefore they should not be regarded in every case, as marking out precise areas of mutually exclusive territory (Cottingham 1984).

LEVELS OF DISCOURSE IN SOCIAL SCIENCE

The levels of discourse are shown on the left hand side of figure 2:1; They are the epistemological, the linguistic (or conceptual) and the ontological. Epistemology can be characterised by its concern with the sources and modes of knowledge, as well as the scope and validity of such knowledge. In sum, epistemology grapples with the question of how we are able to know things. Ontology on the other hand is concerned with the question of *what* are the things we know; what are the objects of our knowledge. I shall use the category of ontology to refer to the general nature of (social) reality as it is described or elucidated in different forms of discourse. There are good philosophical grounds and precedents for construing ontology in this way, although it needs to be noted that some realists and phenomenologists have construed it in a much narrower way. These authors have restricted the meaning of ontology to a concern with 'personal being', that is, reality as experienced and perceived by human beings. I shall use the term ontology in a much wider sense than this to include the idea that social reality may also be constituted by phenomena beyond the ambit of personal being (for example, social structures).

The third level, the linguistic/conceptual is not a level in the same sense as are epistemology and ontology. Whereas epistemology and ontology refer to, and are concerned with, fundamentally different (although related) questions about knowledge and the nature of

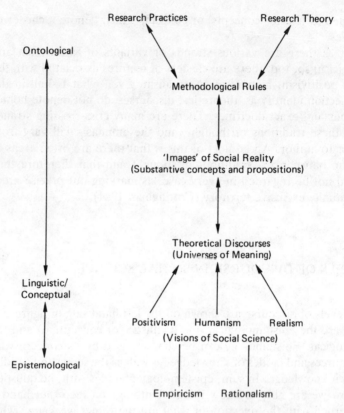

FIGURE 2.1   *Levels and Types of Discourse in Social Science*

things, this level includes reference to both these aspects. Not only does language mediate meaning as such, but in so doing it mediates the interchanges and mutual influences between epistemology and ontology.

This brings me to a crucial point where my formulations move quite away from the standard realist account. Unlike the orthodox realist position, I shall treat epistemological questions as prior to, or more basic than ontological questions, since descriptions of reality are, in some measure, the result of the application of specific epistemological premises. However, the degree of influence will vary with the specific circumstances in question. Of course, social reality exists independently of the terms in which it is expressed as knowledge. It has an external 'substance' (material and/or ideal) which sometimes, and in specific circumstances makes it recalcitrant to inappropriate or incorrect descriptions. Thus, ontological items may 'feed back' and influence the way in which we come to know and understand them.

However, all descriptions of the objects of our knowledge (that is, *what* we know), are *already* ineradicably bound up with specific preconceptions about the nature of our knowledge, that is, how we come to know the things we know (the objects of our knowledge). This statement obviously needs unpacking and I shall be doing this in part in the following discussion. However, this whole issue will arise again in chapters 3 and 5 where I argue against the opposing position adopted by Bhaskar (1979) and Giddens (1984) and others which stresses the priority of ontology. Pointing to the constructional role played by epistemological and theoretical factors does not commit me to an idealist form of analysis whereby 'reality' is understood as nothing more than a reflection of the internal relations between concepts. I am committed to the idea of an objective reality, but I stress that knowledge of this reality presupposes the use of epistemological and conceptual instruments. Thus, my main focus is on the way in which objective reality is differently conceptualised in different discourses.

So then let me spell out how this view compares with the standard realist view. The realist position argues that there is a realm of real objects which exist (and possess powers) independently of our knowledge of them, and that knowledge somehow attempts to represent them. However, unlike my position, the realist tends to view the independently existing reality as the 'prime mover' in this respect because 'the nature of objects and processes (including human behaviour) determines their cognitive and practical possibilities for us'(Bhaskar 1979, p. 31; Sayer 1984, p. 66). This seems to me to undermine the central realist tenet that there can be no ahistorical, asocial and theory neutral *descriptions* of the world. For if it is the nature of objects and processes (that is, ontological features) which *determine* cognitive and practical possibilities then they must reach us as knowledge in a manner which eludes contamination by prior theoretical presuppositions. If ontological features *determine* cognitive possibilities then our cognition must be some kind of isomorphism or correspondence with these ontological features.

My point is that it is only by breaking with this empiricist theory of knowledge that one can understand the way in which epistemological and theoretical factors as socially and historically grounded practices actually influence the *way* in which the independently existing world is *known* to us. Whilst the ontological features of the world may constrain certain aspects of our knowledge (and the different implications for the physical and social worlds are extremely important here) they certainly do not determine our knowledge. This is especially apparent in the social sciences, whereby specific ontological features are mediated by, and thus to some extent constructed by the epistemological, theoretical and methodological discourses in which they are constituted in the first place.

Further on, I shall give examples of the way in which ontological features such as the nature of interaction, the nature of institutions, the nature of power and the concepts of structure, class and role are differently conceptualised within different theoretical (and epistemological) discourses. Realism has not attended to this dimension of knowledge, namely, the way it is constituted within pre-existing theoretical and linguistic universes. In short, the realist position at present is unable to acknowledge that rationalistic elements do influence the cognitive possibilities of the world, precisely because knowledge *is* historically and socially grounded in different traditions (of theory and knowledge).

The framework that I present here attempts to deal with this crucially important dimension of knowledge. Thus, I emphasise the significance of viewing epistemological and theoretical concerns as prior to ontological ones, without viewing knowledge as completely independent.

Thus whilst the linguistic constitution of objects of knowledge *predispose* our cognitive and perceptual apprehensions of them (Whorf 1959) there are varying degrees of 'resistance' to arbitrary inclusion or complete assimilation in a conventionalist manner. First, the established conceptual (home) network imposes constraints upon the ongoing conceptualisation or incorporation of objects. Secondly, depending on their degree of *experiential reference* social objects themselves represent resistances to incorrect depictions arbitrated through sensorily validated 'evidence'. Put another way, social objects of knowledge may be ranged along a continuum between structural (abstract) and experiential (concrete) phenomena. The more they approximate to the structural pole the more exclusively they are subject to the constraints of the home discourse or competing theoretical discourses. The more they approximate to the experiential pole the more subject they will be to the dual influences of established conceptual networks *as well as* sensorily arbitrated evidence.

I shall return to these questions as the discussion unfolds but more particularly in the next chapter. (See chapter 6 also, for a detailed discussion of this issue.) However, before going on I want to suggest that one of the reasons that realists do not attend to these issues is they tend to use examples from the natural physical world as general support for their contention that it is the nature of (physical) objects that 'determines their cognitive possibilities for us'. These examples of physical objects are a source of confusion here because their properties are in no way comparable to social objects and thus are unsatisfactory exemplars for our understanding or knowledge of social phenomena.

THE NOTION OF DISCOURSE

In general terms a discourse refers to a framework and mode of reasoning in which discrete clusterings of concepts are used as linguistic resources with which to answer questions which are posed in terms of these very ideas and concepts. In this sense discourses are relatively integrated networks of concepts (see Hesse 1974, Thomas 1979) which provide the parameters for certain forms of argument and the posing and answering of specific kinds of questions. As such, discrete and coherent 'schools' or traditions of thought such as empiricism, humanism, functionalism, Marxism and so on, can be understood as discourses.

However, the criteria of validity associated with a discourse (say symbolic interactionism), are not simply contained within its overt framework of language and concepts; they are ultimately anchored in its humanist vision of social science and its empiricist epistemological premises. In this sense theoretical and methodological discourses (including research practices) are always penetrated to some degree or other by lower level epistemological discourses which underpin their validity conditions. The validity criteria of discourses are therefore dependent upon a restricted core of epistemological propositions in terms of which all discourses may be compared and evaluated. Thus, I reject complete epistemological relativism in which each discourse possesses exclusively internal criteria of validity and in which there is no possibility of cross-discourse dialogue and no criteria of comparability (see Kuhn 1962, Feyerabend 1975, Hindess and Hirst 1977). The framework presented here is relativistic in the highly circumscribed sense that it envisages more than one possible notion of truth in social scientific matters, and thus departs from the traditional positivist view that one method alone (namely positivism) should monopolise claims to objective truth.

However, discourses do possess some internal criteria which are specific to those discourses. Naturally, different discourses deal with varying 'contents' which constitute as it were, the subject matter and topography of the discourse, and thus some criteria of validity will be governed by what these contents actually are. For example, symbolic interactionism attempts to account for, or explain linguistically mediated social behaviour. Thus, a valid account must be expressed precisely in these terms. A functionalist explanation must be couched in terms of its 'subject matter', that is, the functional interrelationships of social institutions. However, it is also possible for these same discourses to *share* other validity criteria, in this case both symbolic interactionism and functionalism share a general commitment to empiricism.

However, this is not an idealist analysis. The very notion of the contents or objects of a discourse implies both internal and external referents. The internal referents are the concepts or the linguistic means of expression of the discourse itself. The external referents refer to the concrete reality which the concepts and language are meant to describe or symbolise. The internal referents primarily feed into theoretical and methodological construals of discursive 'problems', whilst the external referents are primarily concerned with the practical and substantive dimensions of them, although there are cross-over effects deriving from each type of referent. The problematicity of discourses produces a criss-crossing of theoretical, methodological, political and ideological aspects, some of which may be more influential and produce more important effects within discourses, but none of which can be seen as completely autonomous.

SOCIAL SCIENTIFIC DISCOURSES

Moving up Figure 2.1 we cross the binary line between epistemological and ontological levels of analysis. Here, I first want to demonstrate the usefulness of understanding theoretical schools or frameworks as theoretical *discourses*, as well as differentiating this notion from the more traditional conception of 'theory'. Second, I want to show how theoretical discourses can be understood as universes of meaning constituted through language. Thirdly, I want to show how these universes have implications for ontological concerns including the methods and practice of social research.

SCHOOLS OF THEORY AS THEORETICAL DISCOURSES

In treating schools of theory such as symbolic interactionism, functionalism, structural or humanist Marxism, psychoanalysis, and so forth, as theoretical discourses we move away from the conception of 'a theory' in the narrow positivistic sense of 'a set of logically related hypotheses specifying expected relationships among variables, and open to falsification through evidence drawn from the world' (Stryker 1980, p. 8). The idea of theoretical discourse is much more general than this, but whilst it could be claimed, for example, that symbolic interactionism is not a theory in the narrow sense, to say that it is an approach or a list of interlocked concepts says nothing much about it. The real question is what is it that makes the concepts that constitute it *interlock* in the first place; in essence, what produces its coherence?

Thus, theoretical discourses are relatively discrete clusterings of concepts which provide the internal conditions and theoretical shelter for the posing of certain problems and arbitrating the validity of certain kinds of answer. For example, symbolic interactionism (which includes the concepts of 'self', 'significant symbol', 'generalised other' and so on) poses such problems as 'how is social co-operation possible?' It suggests also an answer; that co-operation is possible because human beings interact with each other via significant symbols, and are thus able to enter into the social roles of others and respond to their needs and demands. The validity of these and other questions and answers formulated by symbolic interactionism is arbitrated in terms of its predominately humanist vision of social science and its empiricist epistemological premises.

Similarly, functionalism poses the problem of why certain institutions exist in societies, answers it in terms of the social functions performed by these institutions, and validates these answers in terms of a positivist vision of social science and an empiricist theory of knowledge. Structural Marxism also poses problems in terms of its conceptual framework. For example, the problem of social change is both posed and answered in terms of concepts such as the 'forces and relations of production', 'class domination', 'contradictions' in the capitalist mode of production and so on. Validity is gauged in terms of a realist vision of social science and a rationalist epistemology.

It is instructive to view such conceptual networks as universes of meaning constituted through language. Whorf (1959) demonstrates that cognition and perception are to a large extent built up through the use of language, and that differences in language between cultures and subcultures generate differences in 'world view' by providing different linguistic categories and structures with which to characterise these worlds. Thus, quite basic concepts such as time, space and the like, are tied to quite different views of the world through the linguistic mediations of different cultures. In a similar way theoretical discourses provide conceptual totalities with which to characterise the world of objects which they seek to account for or explain.

A discourse and its community of users (or the originator, if there is only one user) becomes the holistic context in which the specific linguistic and conceptual items gain meaning. Such meanings can only vary (if at all) within the limits imposed by the discourse itself. Unlike the linguistic relativity hypothesis, however, the meaning-confering units of language are not seen as elements of a somewhat arbitrary system of natural language categories but are, rather, treated as a function of the holistic or organic nature of the theoretical discourse itself. The point of the comparison then is to highlight the way in which language either as a naturally occurring system or as a 'constructed' network is generative of specific cognitive and perceptual universes.

Two things are being implied here. First, the idea that the different conceptual networks or clusters constitute different orderings of social reality or society can be seen quite simply in the evocations of these things in the language of the different discourses. For example, the language of symbolic interactionism describes the ways in which people co-operate with each other through interaction via the use of significant symbols; how identities are negotiated and selves developed; how social life can be metaphorically compared with a theatrical drama, and so on. The language of Marxism invokes such things as the class nature of capitalist society, antagonistic relations of domination and coercion, dehumanisation at the workplace, and the like. The language of functionalism stresses institutional interdependence of social functions in the division of labour and the 'natural' and universal development of status hierarchies.

Secondly, the idea that specific concepts gain their meaning only in relation to the conceptual totality can be seen in the example of the concept of class. In Marxism the concept of class expresses a particular relation of power and control over the means of production, whilst in functionalism the concept of class (if the word is used at all) is synonymous with some ordinal scale of remuneration in the occupational status structure. Another example, the concept of role in symbolic interactionism is used much more in the dramaturgical sense of a social or theatrical performance of a script, whereas in functionalism it is used rather more as an expression or means of institutional functioning, that is, as the smallest unit of social structure.

The network and meaning universe conceptions of discourse are not meant to imply consensus within their parameters, but rather to convey the boundary defining functions of the linguistic/conceptual structure of a discourse *vis-à-vis* other discourses, for example, symbolic interactionism versus functionalism versus structural Marxism, rather than the distinctions within discourses.

METHODOLOGICAL AND RESEARCH DISCOURSES: THE PRACTICE OF SOCIAL RESEARCH

I have concentrated upon describing how theoretical discourses represent important conduits between the epistemological premises of differing conceptions of social science and linguistically mediated and influenced evocations of social reality. At this ontological level, methodological and practical research discourses are linked to theoretical discourses (and ultimately to epistemological discourses) in that the latter are associated with different research traditions. Thus, sociological and psychological approaches such as functionalism or experimental social psychology have favoured research methods such as surveys, the analysis of official statistics or laboratory experiments, in which there is a high degree of control over research variables and a primary emphasis on quantitative data. This is because they share a common positivist empiricist basis which demands rigour and objectivity in the manipulation of variables and the quest for causal correlations.

Other theoretical discourses, such as the Chicago school of symbolic interactionism or certain humanist psychologies, have *tended* to emphasise less impersonal methods, such as participant observation, as a result of their attempts to come to terms with aspects of the subjective and interactional experiences of human beings. This had led to the development of methods and strategies designed to elicit the collection of qualitative forms of data. Again, these aspects are directly connected to the humanist and empiricist foundations of these discourses.

Just as important as the existence of organic links between methodological, theoretical and epistemological discourses is the matter of the way in which different conceptions of what I shall term 'research theory' are associated with different clusterings of discourses or elements of discourses. 'Research theory' differs from theoretical discourse in that is specifies the form in which theory must emerge from the process of research itself. Thus, conceptions of 'research theory' are contained within, and are constrained by, clusters of discursive (including theoretical discourse) parameters. For example, Merton's notion of 'middle-range theory' is very definitely to be located within positivist empiricism and the research practices associated with these discourses. The term 'ground theory' has been used to describe a form of research theory in the humanist tradition (Glaser and Strauss 1967) although there are variants (see Layder 1982).

THE PLACE OF REALISM IN THE ANALYSIS OF DISCOURSE

It is in relation to the questions of methodology, research theory and research practices that one can begin to understand the realist position as rather distinct from the other discursive positions and their interconnections. Realism has no distinct methodological position of its own which is in turn underpinned by a definite theoretical position. In this sense realism has appropriated already established theoretical and methodological positions and claimed them for itself. This has led to a number of confusions and ambiguities in the realist project.

Methodologically, realist writers if drawn at all on this issue have seemed to endorse two sorts of thing. The first is derived from the realist critique of the presupposition of a closed system in positivist type research, which typically employs large-scale surveys or representive samples of populations and uses formal questionnaires, standardised interviews and statistical analyses in an effort to map the relationship between 'causal' variables. This is viewed by realists as producing predominantly descriptive and representative generalis-ations, but which lack explanatory depth. Thus, Harré (1979, 1981) and Sayer (1984) have proposed 'intensive' research designs as opposed to the 'extensive' ones of positivism. In intensive designs the focus is on how some causal process works out in a particular case or a limited number of cases and the favoured methods are causal analysis, participant observation and/or informal and interac-tive interviews. In short, intensive studies employ qualitative as opposed to quantitative methods.

There is, of course, nothing new in the methodological prescrip-tions of Harré and Sayer; participant observation and interactive interviews have been part and parcel of the symbolic interactionist literature for some considerable time (Becker 1970, Glaser and Strauss 1967) whilst ethnographic methods in sociology have also been propounded by many ethnomethodologists. What is new in the notion of intensive research is that these established methodologies with their theoretical attachments have been reconceptualised as serving realist social scientific objectives. Thus, whereas the notions of (generative) structure and causality are anathema to symbolic interactionism and ethnomethodology they have been reintroduced and cemented to methodologies which were designed as radical alter-natives to the scientific paradigm.

In terms of the present framework it is clear that this kind of unreflective and wholesale appropriation of methods which were originally designed for quite other ends, leads to problems in and for the coherence of the realist project. In particular, the problem of the unwitting importation of empiricist limitations on knowledge is crucial. As I mentioned in chapter 1, the realist assumption that empiricism has been abandoned with the banishment of positivism is ill-founded in the light of the empiricist geneology of so-called 'intensive' research designs. Whilst the humanist traditions have always disavowed the scientistic search for external causal generalis-ations and variables and the generation of falsifiable hypotheses and predictive laws, nonetheless, they have concurred with positivism over the epistemological assumption of empiricism.

That is to say, whilst adopting a different vision of social analysis (namely, that it is a 'science') and attaching itself to different theories (holism, functionalism, behaviourism, holistic eclecticism) and quite different research methodologies (large-scale survey research, the laboratory experiment), positivism is allied with humanism over the question of the basic source and mode of knowledge – empiricism. Both humanism and positivism agree on the sensory limitations of knowledge and exclude any rationalistic forms of validity and theoretical knowledge. It is precisely this tie which is largely, if not wholly, unacknowledged by realism and which produces a similar empiricist bias in realism. Realism cannot afford to have its explanatory power narrowed in this way. The break with positivism must occur at its tap root of epistemological assumptions, otherwise it simply reproduces the same limitations. It is not enough to appropriate more 'palatable' theories (of a humanist persuasion) and relabel them as realist.

In the next chapter I will attempt to specify how and in what sense realism should admit of rationalistic modes of explanation and validity whilst not completely 'writing off' empiricist knowledge. I would claim that this represents a much more 'honest' approach to empiricism. Instead of the current realist orthodoxy of assuming that the problems of empiricism have been transcended (for example see Harré 1979), the present framework attempts to specify the limits of empiricism (whilst utilising its indubitably important insights) and to go beyond them by engaging with 'moderate' forms of rationalism (see the next chapter).

Another theoretical/methodological preference displayed by some realists is in many respects quite contrary to this notion of 'intensive qualitative' research design. In this respect Bhaskar seems to view variants of Marxism as the exemplar of successful realist social science. Certainly, while some aspects of the Marxist project serve well as illustrations of what might be thought of as 'generative mechanisms', there is no indication how the Marxist project fits into a clear methodological conception of research practice. Certainly, if realism eschews positivist survey research then there are only two options for it. Either it takes up the option of intensive qualitative research or it creates a third alternative.

Now the possibility of joining Marxian structural conceptions of social processes with intensive research design is a tantalising possibility even though this has not been started yet with any systematic attention to the epistemological and theoretical problems involved. Certainly, one possibility would be simply to ignore these problems and throw Marxist theory and intensive research together without heed of the result. However, this would indeed produce an unsatisfactory and unprincipled eclecticism.

The other option for the Marxist brand of realism would be to strike out on its own. But the question still remains what would an empirical research project look like? Would it look very different from the extensive research designs of positivism? Would it retreat into a form of Althusserian theoretical practice? Such programmatic statements as there are, are characteristically (and frustratingly) vague and idealistic (for instance, Sayer's notion of critical theory as having an 'emancipatory' focus, 1984, pp. 229–34).

CONCLUSION

My intention in the foregoing has been to present a framework wherein the realist project can be mapped onto the topography of extant social scientific practices viewed as levels and types of discourse. This stratified view of social science is entirely consonant with the realist programme but hitherto has not been attempted in realist writing.

Specifically, the framework underwrites the idea that the objects of social scientific knowledge exist independently of our knowledge of them, another theorem of realism. However, the framework departs from realist orthodoxy in that it insists that our knowledge of this external world is not simply given to us in the nature of these objects. That is, this framework rejects the view that the cognitive possibilities of objects are determined by their nature. Any other position would be to turn a blind eye to the historical specificity of the variegated forms of knowledge that exist in different social scientific discourses. It is precisely these forms and the realists' relation to them that is mapped by the framework.

I have adopted a contrary view to realism by stressing the priority of epistemological matters and underwriting the constructional and predispositional role of theory and the constitutive language of theory. In the next chapter I shall develop this argument further and trace through the consequences for the validity claims of realism. However, it remains to be reiterated that if realism can be understood as being able to sustain the kind of framework presented herein, then it should be able to understand its relation to positivism and humanism in a more detailed and productive way by tracing through the interconnections between the different levels of social scientific discourses.

3 Realism and Validity Claims

THE EMPIRICIST-RATIONALIST CONTINUUM

As I intimated in the previous chapter, I think that realism should take seriously the debate between empiricism and rationalism with a view to obtaining a precise estimation of where it stands in the debate. In what follows I characterise the relationship between empiricism and rationalism as a continuum in terms of which one can situate particular kinds of knowledge (or discourse) according to their differing degrees of commitment to each of these forms (and modes of acquisition) of knowledge. In this sense the following discussion complements the analysis of discourses presented in the foregoing chapter by concentrating on the epistemological presuppositions of the discourses. The importance of the scheme that I will outline concerns the evaluation of the explanatory powers of different discourses or forms of knowledge and in particular the explanatory power of realist knowledge in relation to other forms. I shall deal with these as issues relating to the *validity* claims of realism further on, but I shall begin by defining what I mean by empiricism and rationalism.

NAIVE AND SOPHISTICATED EMPIRICISM

There is, of course, a great difference between 'empiricism' as a mode of knowledge and the 'empirical world' as a possible object of knowledge. If this distinction is made, it is clear that knowledge of the empirical world may be empiricist or non-empiricist (rationalist). There is no necessary correlation between a concern with the empirical world (that is, a world beyond theoretical discourse) and empiricism, a doctrine which insists on the sensory limitations of knowledge, that is, that the objects of theory are the given, phenomenal, experienced objects in the world and that theory must be proven or falsified in relation to them.

However, the problem of empiricism in sociology and social psychology has hardly been confronted because it is often assumed that there is only one species of empiricism to be found, namely, the naive variety. This leaves out of account what I term 'sophisticated' empiricism of which there are many forms, although here I shall deal with one major form which permeates much social research.

Popper (1959, p. 106) identifies the naive empiricist as one who believes that science begins with the scientist's presuppositionless observation of the world and progresses with the establishment of knowledge by the accumulation, through controlled observation, of the objectively verified 'facts' of the world. More sophisticated empiricists, however, establish distance between themselves and the naive view in one or both of the following ways. First (and in accord with Popper's own view) such empiricists might assert that observations cannot be made without the intervention of theoretical presuppositions; that in a sense all observations are theory-laden. In this case it is not the intervention of presuppositions which prevents knowledge from becoming 'scientific knowledge; rather, the demarcation criterion that distinguishes science from non-science turns on the potential falsifiability of scientific theories. That is, the logical form of scientific theories must be such that they are open to empirical refutation. Lakatos (1972) has extended Popper's falsification thesis in so far as the original emphasis on a single falsifying observation as the arbiter of the validity of a theory has been supplanted by the idea that falsification only properly occurs when a 'discarded' theory is replaced by one which has greater explanatory power. With relation to sociological and social psychological theory, it suffices to say that these disciplines have been, and continue to be influenced by the notion that theories should be 'open to falsification through evidence drawn from the world' (Stryker 1980, p. 8).

In the above sense 'sophisticated' falsificationism becomes a sophisticated empiricism, since it ultimately relies on recourse to observations or experience as the final arbiters of the validity of knowledge as opposed to rational forms of proof and demonstration. Of course, to say that sociology and social psychology have been heavily influenced by these notions of falsifiability is not to claim that all practitioners are concerned with the specific notion of falsifiability as an integral feature of their methodological and theoretical prescriptions. Elias (1978), for example, attempts to move away from the notion of a universal logic of discovery to a position in which the historical emergence of different forms of scientific knowledge becomes the focus of analysis. Viewed in this light, Elias claims that the relationship between new findings and older knowledge in science cannot be expressed in terms of 'static polarities' like 'true' and 'false'; rather, 'theoretical and empirical knowledge becomes more extensive, more correct, and more adequate' (p. 53). Of course, this contextualisation and relativisation of the problem in no way dispenses with the fundamental issue that Popper was concerned with; that is, what criteria (or criterion) of validity separates out scientific statements from non-scientific statements at any specific historical juncture and particularly *after* the emergence of the modern Western form of science.

That this is a problem that will not go away as Elias wishes it would, is exemplified in the very language that he uses as a purported alternative to the so-called static polarities of 'true and false'. To say that knowledge becomes 'more correct and more adequate' does not rid one of polarities; to say that something is 'more correct' is also to state that something can be 'incorrect' or 'more correct' which sets up a polarity remarkably similar to the standards of truth and falsity which Elias seeks to transcend. Of course, to talk of something being 'more true' or 'more false' no more resolves the problem of what constitutes the moment at which something becomes true rather than false, that is, how someone decides or classifies something as false rather than true and vice versa. Similarly, to talk of something being 'more adequate' is nothing more than ambiguous word play, if no standards are laid down specifying how adequacy relates to inadequacy.

Predictably enough, however, there are ultimate standards of scientificity in Elias' schema, and again, far from being at odds with positivist empiricist standards there is a remarkable concurrence in that 'factual observation' is the final arbiter of scientific truth:

> scientists are destroyers of myths. By factual observation, they endeavour to replace myths, religious ideas, metaphysical speculations and all unproven images of natural processes with theories – testable, verifiable and correctable by factual observation. (1978, p. 52)

In this scheme the notion of falsifiability is omitted whilst the positivist empiricist criteria of testability, verifiability and correctability through 'factual observation' are endorsed. Thus, Elias' position grounds itself in an empiricist theory of knowledge. Of course, not all discussions of the place and role of theory and method in the generation of knowledge self-consciously espouse a specific philosophy of science. It is more generally the case that whilst engaged in either exegetical, or original substantive work sociologists and social psychologists 'make do' with rather vague and woolly formulations about the importance of induction and the 'reciprocal' influence of theory and observation. For example, Stryker (1980, p. 13) states:

> The business of science. . . . is a never-ending process of moving from observations to possible explanations to observations *ad infinitum*.

Even in the absence of systematic discussions of the nature of explanation and the specification of the exact relationship between explanations and observations (including how one proceeds from one to the other), we are left in no doubt that the *apparently* undogmatic attitude of 'a dash of observation and a dash of explanation equals scientific knowledge' is quite firmly committed to an empiricist conception. This is so because it assumes that observation is not only the guarantor of valid explanation but also, in this case, the initial source of knowledge and, as such, excludes any form of *a priori* or partially autonomous, rational or theoretical criteria of validity.

RATIONALISM

As is the case with empiricism (and as if have emphasised at other junctures), there are several different strands of thought associated with the term rationalism. Since I am not concerned with some of these it is necessary to be clear about what they are. The strict philosophical sense of the term rationalism must be distinguished from two non-technical usages. First, the idea that it implies a 'rational' view of the world as against a theistic of supernatural outlook must be dispensed with. Similarly, there is no *necessary* connection between the notion of rationalism in the strict sense and the belief that one should reject the notion of some 'deeper' intuitive non-rational form of knowledge.

Whilst rationalism does not necessarily imply these, on a general level it is committed to the idea of reason as a necessary prerequisite of any argument which is concerned with making truth claims. In this sense all philosophy is rationalist. However, rationalism as I use it is not synonymous with the notion of reason operating in accordance with formal rational principles such as formal logic or mathematics. Whilst rationalism may at some junctures be concerned with

these things, in the present context I shall be dealing with rationalism
as a general epistemological posture which concerns itself with the
function of theory and theoretical frameworks in the determination
of knowledge. In this respect formal and mathematical logic take
back seat to the contextually specific logics that all social scientific
discourses possess.

It can be argued that all rationalists possess (in the technical sense)
a commitment to *a priori* knowledge, that is, to the idea that the
truth of propositions can be established independently of sensory
observation. Whilst I share this commitment to the central importance of *a priori* knowledge, I would wish to stress that I do not see an
absolute gulf between *a priori* knowledge and sensory observation. I
would prefer to stress the proposition that the internal relations of
concepts in a discourse play an *extremely important role* not only in
the formation of the 'perceptual sets' which guide observations, but
also in arbitrating the validity of observational and theoretical propositions emanating from the discourse.

It is this specific focus of interest which distinguishes my own
concerns from those of other rationalists who share a commitment
to *a priori* knowledge. In this respect I shall not be concerned with
those strands of rationalism which have been termed 'innatism' and
'necessitarianism'. As far as innatism is concerned, my usage of the
term rationalism is not linked with any claim about the innate features of the human mind, such that it possesses reasoning faculties
through which it can reach 'true' conclusions about the world. Nor
am I suggesting that the human mind already possesses an inherent
or deep structure which predisposes it to interpret experience in a
certain way. (Chomsky has brought about a modern revival of this
kind of Leibnizian innatism in relation to language acquisition.)

Necessitarianism is a strand of rationalism which emphasises the
search for, and the uncovering of, necessary truths about reality. My
position on this is that the idea of necessary truths about the real
world cannot be sustained if this is taken to mean that the properties
attaching to real things in the world can be known to us entirely
independently of an epistemological and theoretical infrastructure,
that is, as if these truths were 'essences' which somehow represent
themselves to us as pristine truths. In what amounts to much the
same thing but in a different form of words, I would argue that the
idea of a necessary truth cannot be sustained if it is taken to refer
to irreducible ontological features of the (social) world which are

assumed to determine our knowledge of them. (See later discussion of Bhaskar on ontology.)

THE OBJECTIVES OF THE PROPOSED CONTINUUM

Having defined what I mean by the terms empiricism and rationalism, I want now to consider the usefulness of the idea of a continuum between the two. This can be expressed in the form of two related points. First, such a continuum may help us go beyond debates about the ultimate validity of forms of knowledge conceived of as an opposition between truth and untruth, as in the debate between empiricist versus rationalist forms of knowledge or as implied in the debate between 'scientific' and 'metaphysical' explanations. The type of black and white debates which set out to prove that either rationalism is worthless and vacuous (Ayer 1971, Rock 1979, Bruyn 1966) or that empiricism is a baseless pseudo-science (D. and J. Willer 1973; Althusser 1969; Hindess and Hirst 1977) do not do justice to the complexity and subtlety of the issues involved.

For example, the distinction that the latter group of authors makes between 'science' and 'empiricism' whereby most of sociology and social psychology is empiricist and therefore, in their terms, 'unscientific' (and hence irredeemably wrong), leaves out of account the possibility of conceiving of (a) definite and quite different strands within social theory and research practices, and (b) (as a result) conceiving of the possibility of different degrees of, and approximations to, 'science (rationalism in their terms) and 'empiricism' in relation to the different schools.

On the other hand, those working within the empiricist tradition have also perpetuated this kind of black and white, 'all or nothing' debate by making two main types of response to the brute fact of empiricism. One response has been to omit to discuss it as an important or genuinely problematic issue and to get on with the business of generating knowledge from within an already accredited and entrenched discourse (for instance, symbolic interactionism, ethnomethodology, functionalism, conflict theory, and so on). The second main response to empiricism has been to actively and explicitly embrace it as the only true and valid means of attaining knowledge of the social world (Rock 1979; Bruyn 1966). This, of course, is the opposite extreme to that of the critics of empiricism. Empiricism itself is asserted to be the only true province and means of attaining scientific knowledge and thus, the major problems of validity are those associated with non-empiricist forms of knowledge.

As I have said before, a primary reason why these forms of non-response to the critique of empiricism exist, concerns the fact that many sociologists and social psychologists consider either that the problem has been solved or that their disciplines have progressively rid themselves of the problem. Thus, many sociologists and social psychologists invoke the Popperian idea of demarcation criteria between true 'scientific knowledge' and 'metaphysical speculation'. In this case true scientific knowledge of the social is differentiated from metaphysical speculation (including rationalist forms of knowledge) by criteria of falsifiability and testability, and the like. Scientific knowledge is also differentiated from what Popper calls naive empiricism by the assertion of the importance of the role of theory in the ordering of observations. Merton has endorsed this position in his call for middle-range systematic theory in sociology.

Thus, by a certain amount of casuistry many of the social sciences manage to escape the problem of empiricism by subsuming them all under the rubric of 'naive empiricism' which they claim to transcend, and which, for the most part, they do. Also, these disciplines assert their scientific character by rendering rational forms of knowledge redundant, or declaring them to be metaphysical nonsense because of inherent unfalsifiability or lack of testability, or seeming irrelevance. What such arguments conceal is the fact that much sociology and social psychology operates in terms of a sophisticated empiricism with all its attendant limitations.

Thus, by asserting and operating through different definitions of 'science' and 'scientificity' both the critics of empiricism and empiricists themselves are able to displace responsibility for the problems of knowledge and pin it on their adversaries. As I have implied, it is the extreme and dogmatic nature of the formulations of those who have criticised empiricism within social science that has often prevented acceptance of, and response to, important aspects of the critique of empiricism. Similarly, a steadfast refusal to admit to the possibility of valid non-empiricist forms and criteria of knowledge by some social scientists has led to an inability to perceive the potential fruitfulness of some aspects of these alternatives.

The second point concerning the potential usefulness of the idea of an empiricist-rationalist continuum relates to the objective of moving away from the inflexibility and inaccuracy of bald oppositions such as 'empiricism' versus 'science' and 'science' versus 'metaphysics' which imply some contrast between truth and falsity. To do this we must bear in mind that there are competing versions of 'scientific' knowledge within social science which are constituted and legitimated by those clusters of discourses that I identified in the foregoing chapters. I propose therefore that we must assess the competing claims in terms of some metacriterion, *not* of 'true scientificity' (because as we have seen the meaning of 'science' or 'valid knowledge' varies between discursive clusters) but in terms of the degree to which they resolve what I call the restriction problems of extreme empiricism or rationalism.

That is, the degree to which different claims to validity satisfy the (two) following criteria: (a) the extent to which they circumvent the restrictive nature of both naive and sophisticated forms of empiricism by some appreciation of the rational properties of discourses and the place of rational forms of proof and demonstration in knowledge; and (b) the extent to which they avoid the equally restrictive nature of extreme or naive rationalism and incorporate a notion of extra theoretical reference. That is, the degree to which they are able to 'save the phenomena' in Van Fraasen's (1980) terms.

Thus, one replaces an all or nothing notion of scientificity à la Popper (when he dismisses the theories of Marx and Freud as metaphysical nonsense), with the notion of scientific practices as ranging along a continuum of degrees of empiricism or rationalism. In this way, different discourses within sociology and social psychology produce quite different positions in relation to the empiricism-rationalism distinction, as do different levels of analysis within discourses. As a result, instead of constant claims to validity for one's own position and thus attacking the validity of all others, one evaluates theoretical and research discourses around the empiricist-rationalist axis in terms of the degree to which they resolve the respective problems outlined above. Thus, from being something of an 'all or nothing' debate about the 'more correct' form of knowledge or procedure for producing knowledge, the issue can be transformed into what kinds of claims are being made about, and what limitations are being placed upon, substantive and theoretical knowledge in terms of the kinds of problems that are posed by, and thus made possible within, different discursive universes.

THE ROLE OF OBSERVATION AND THE INTRANSITIVE
REALM IN REALISM

What I have so far referred to as levels and types of discursive
practice within social science belong to what Bhaskar (1979) calls
the 'transitive dimension' (extant, cognitive materials of science),
although he and other realists do not analyse these discursive aspects,
and thus fail to appreciate their importance. Instead, they focus on
what Bhaskar calls the 'intransitive' objects of knowledge, that is,
those objects of our knowledge which, it is claimed, 'exist and act
independently of the knowledge of which they are the objects' (1979,
p. 14). That is, the realist is concerned with describing the supposedly
irreducible, and transcendentally real, ontological features that exist
prior to, and independently of, our knowledge of them. I shall try
to show that this latter idea is mistaken, and that a lack of focus on
the wider concerns of theoretical discourse (particularly its 'constructional' role) in certain realist writers, has resulted in their acceding
ontology (the 'real') itself a privileged position. In this sense, their
versions of realism fail to resolve the restriction problems of empiricism as outlined in the previous section.

Keat and Urry's work exemplifies the view that there is an independent ontological realm of real objects which scientific theory
describes. Thus Keat (1971, pp. 6–7) describes realists as 'discovering
the causal mechanisms by which (undoubtedly existent) "theoretical
entitites" bring about the regularities of observable phenomena'. Or
again, 'The realists have insisted that no apparent ontological priority
of observation statements should lead us to deny the ontological
status of entities referred to by terms in the theoretical language'
(Keat 1971, p. 7).

Now whilst it must be granted that one must move away from the
notion of an observation language if we are to avoid the imputation
of ontological privilege, the idea that we have actually moved away
from this position through a concentration upon ontology, that is,
the reality of causal mechanisms referred to by theory, is premature,
if we scrutinise Keat's statements about the relations between theory
and observation. For example, in attempting to break away from the
positivist idea that a statement's scientificity depends upon whether
it is possible to ascertain its truth or falsity by means of direct
observation, Keat and Urry (1975, p. 38) offer an 'alternative' principle: 'a statement is scientific only if it is possible to make observations that would count in some way for its truth or falsity'. How

this position differs from Popper's principle that a scientific statement must be potentially falsifiable, is not clear, although the authors seem in some disagreement with Popper in their discussion of 'conventionalism'.

In these terms it is not really clear what the essential difference is between these two criteria of scientificity. It seems that whilst one could sustain the argument that there is an apparent discontinuity in terms of the imputed source of theoretical (scientific) meaning in these two statements, this is compromised by a similar appeal to observation as the arbiter of the validity of meaning. Thus, whereas in the positivist version the 'meaning' of a scientific statement is given directly via its means of verification, the realist version posits the idea that theoretical entities already have meaning independently of, or prior to, observation. However, since for Keat and Urry the meaning of a theoretical term is only valid (scientific), if it is possible to make observations that would count in some way for or against its truth or falsity, then this would entail the idea of changing or replacing theoretical terms or theories if they were found to be false in terms of observational criteria. Thus, ultimately, observation is the final arbiter of scientificity. This sort of position has great affinities with empiricism whereby given observable, 'real' entities are instrumental in setting the terms for their theoretical depiction. This aspect of the formulation is confirmed in Keat's (1971, p. 7) description of the relations between theoretical terms and observations: 'Rather than attempt to define theoretical terms in observational ones, observations should be seen as giving us *the means of identifying the presence and nature* of unobservable entities' (my emphasis).

This statement reveals the contradictory ambiguity of attempting to avoid the definition of theoretical terms by observational ones whilst at the same time suggesting that observational methods will give us the means of identifying the presence and nature of unobservable entities designated by theoretical terms. If observational methods are to give the means of identifying the presence or absence (and thus, the truth or falsity) of unobservable entities, then how are they to do this other than by providing theoretical definitions of such entities through the use of (some kind of) observation language and associated correspondence rules? In fact Keat and Urry go on to make a very similar point about the function of correspondence rules in realism. That is, correspondence rules for the realist, 'suggest ways of indirectly testing the truth or falsity of theoretical statements; or means by which the presence or absence of the items denoted by theoretical terms can be observationally detected or inferred' (Keat and Urry 1976, p. 38).

The difficulty here can also be seen when one moves from a formal statement of the role and function of observation (and correspondence rules) in realism to a discussion of substantive issues such as 'social class' (Keat and Urry, pp. 93–5). If, as Keat and Urry (and realists in general) state, the unobservable structures and mechanisms that realism identifies, stand behind and produce 'the concrete features of social reality' (p. 135), how can one extrapolate backwards and infer these unobservable mechanisms from specific observations? With the notion of 'class', for instance, Keat and Urry contrast (what they define as) Marx's realist usage of the term class as 'social entities which are not directly observable, but which are historically present', with the positivist usage. In positivism 'analysis is made of the various dimensions along which the individual is located', such as inequalities of income, wealth, status or educational opportunity. Keat and Urry state that for the realist 'the existence of classes is not to be identified with the existence of such inequalities' (pp. 94–5).

I would not want to disagree with this particular construal of a theoretical divide in class analysis, but I would point out that it raises considerable problems and points of contention for the issues discussed previously. Specifically, if observations and correspondence rules are understood to be means of identifying the presence (and/or absence) and nature of unobservable entities and theoretical terms, then how can they do this in terms of the above characterisation of positivist and realist approaches to class? For example, what observations would count as validating the notion of class in a realist sense? Certainly, if class cannot be identified with the more or less observable inequalities, then observations of inequalities cannot identify the presence or absence of classes in a realist sense. If observations in themselves could do this, then again what sorts of observations would count as validating ones?

What seems to be missing from Keat and Urry's formal statements about the relation between theory and observation (and correspondence rules) in realism is some notion of the way in which different theoretical discourses, networks of concepts, and so on, and their underpinning epistemological bases, determine the status of (a) observation in general, considered in relation to a specific body of concepts, and (b) specific observations. If the notion of scientificity is always hedged in by the arbitration of observation tests of truth or falsity, presence or absence, and the like, there is no sense in which there can be a relative autonomy of theory; no realm no matter how circumscribed, of theoretical problems which is a property of theoretical discourse itself, and which determines the status of observation in general or in specific instances. That is, there is no notion of how theoretical discourses act as filters ruling out some observations and ruling in others, as confirming and disconfirming 'evidence'. In the absence of such a notion the theoretical problematics of such a realism are referentially tied to a world whose structure is limited to its supposedly neutral, and objectively real existential/ontological features. Thus, such an epistemology is wedded to a sophisticated empiricist conception whereby the domain of scientific knowledge is conceived as being informed by, and coterminous with, the given (existential, real, phenomenal) structure of the world itself.

More generally my point is that 'observation' and 'observational means' cannot be viewed as some independent appropriation of the ontological and real features of the social world even if we assume that such appropriations are guided by 'realist criteria'. It is this latter assumption which seems to be the heart of the matter; because one has adopted a formal realist position on the nature of social science this somehow transforms the status of observations made under its aegis. Clearly, by employing realist criteria *per se* one can only etch the broad parameters of explanatory adequacy. For instance, one can describe in general terms the *sort* of explanation one is looking for, namely, one that employs the notion of generative mechanisms, and so forth. However, as I have tried to argue in previous chapters, if it is the case that even the broad parameters have a contestable quality about them then they provide no certainty or precision. Such is the case with the empiricist-rationalist debate; as long as there are fundamental equivocations on this issue then the search for generative mechanisms cannot be taken to be the self-explanatory template of realist explanation. Rather, how one gains knowledge of structures will affect to some extent the ontological and explanatory status of these structures.

However, more specifically, the particular shape and form of these structures do not 'emerge out of "primordial" social reality' as if untouched by human knowledge. Operationally and existentially independant of our cognising experience they may be, but the elementary structures of the world never escape the net of language and knowledge, as *our* knowledge. We can never intellectually know the world in its pristine or raw state, because this would demand some pre-linguistic intuitive 'knowledge'. But the knowledge that scientists (and realists) are interested in is discursive knowledge, not that of intuition, and, of necessity discursive knowledge is linguistically constituted. Thus, it can never be unsullied observation of the world that can produce knowledge of generative structures. Instead, we must look to the background theoretical context that is being employed to understand the world.

This is the case with realist invocations of Marxist notions of class, for example. It is the overall theoretical structure of Marxism, not the meta-methodology of realism, which gives meanings to a concept such as class and differentiates it from the 'stratification' version. Observations which were employed to validate the notion of class in either sense would be guided by the theoretical terms in which they are meaningfully constituted (they would not and could not be guided by totally neutral observational means because they are already meaningfully constituted). This theoretical underpinning determines which observational evidence counts as evidence for or against the model, and this is indeed the reason for the co-existence of competing ideas such as 'class' versus 'stratification' in the first place.

Now again the question of adjudicating between such theories is not a matter of invoking observation-neutral criteria since this is impossible, but rather, depends on two things. First, invoking epistemological criteria of validity – such as the degree to which theoretical discourses resolve the restriction problems of empiricism and rationalism and thus have greater explanatory scope. Second, developing interstitial conceptual networks which could facilitate inter-theory communication and thus feed into adjudication between competing claims. This, of course, would depend upon the prior outcome of the first point – the assessment of explanatory adequacy and scope in epistemological terms. It would also require epistemological judgements as to the commensurability or otherwise of specific concepts or whole segments of the conceptual network. Now the problems attending the development of inter-theory communication may prove to be too great in specific circumstances, but the point I am making still stands: adjudication could only be achieved by employing meta-theoretical criteria, it could not be achieved by appeal to some fictive notion of neutral observational means.

PRACTICAL ADEQUACY AND TRUTH

Another, although related strand in realist writing has proposed that the concept of truth should be replaced by the concept of practical adequacy (A. Sayer 1984; D. Sayer 1979; Bhaskar 1979) This in turn is connected to the notion of ontological priority in realism. However, I shall deal with the latter issue as it appears in the writing of Bhaskar and Giddens in due course, whilst here I want to comment on some of the general implications of the idea of practical adequacy as a replacement of the notion of truth since I feel that such a proposal contains some formidable weaknesses.

Sayer (1984) makes an argument for the practical adequacy of knowledge by contrasting it with what he takes to be a conventionalist view of knowledge. According to Sayer the error of conventionalism is 'to ignore practice and the structure of the world' (p. 66); thus knowledge is fickle and haphazard and can be changed at the collective will. On this view knowledge and the world are whatsoever we care to make them. Contrary to this, the realist position insists that knowledge must be practically adequate to its object, that is, it 'must generate expectations about the world and about the results of our actions which are actually realised' (p. 66).

Sayer gives the example of two statements, one to the effect that 'we cannot walk on water' and the other to the effect that 'we can'. The first is more practically adequate since it generates expectations which are realised, that is, we find that we cannot in fact walk on water. In turn it is the *nature* of water which determines its cognitive possibilities for us and therefore its practical adequacy. Thus, Sayer suggests 'why not simply say. . . . that knowledge can only be judged as more or less useful' than true or false? 'That the usefulness is not accidental but due to the nature of the objects of knowledge' (p. 66).

I shall deal with the question of whether the nature of the objects of our knowledge determines their cognitive possibilities for us presently, but let me first focus on the call to substitute practical adequacy for truth. In so far, and only in so far as Sayer wishes to dispense with the notions of truth as exemplified in the positivist and conventionalist views, then I would register some kind of agreement; however, I disagree fundamentally that we abolish the notion of truth completely. I agree that the positivist view of truth as the expression of a correspondence between concepts or theories and the 'facts' or 'objects' which they represent is inadequate and leads to an absolutist and monopolistic stance on knowledge. Similarly, a radically conventionalist position in which the relation between internal and external referents of a discourse were totally abitrary and changeable at will would not do justice to the structures and mechanisms of the world which *operate* independently of our knowledge of them.

However, this state of affairs calls for a different approach to truth, not an abandonment of the notion! The idea of practical adequacy is such a limpid substitute and opens the door to all sorts of opinions, assumptions and ideas. Furthermore, whilst practical adequacy may have some validity in the context of examples found in the natural world (for instance, the example of water) when we come to consider its implications for social reality it begins to collapse completely.

The most serious drawback to the notion of practical adequacy is that it completely ignores cognitive claims to validity. Cognitive adequacy no longer has a role to play in arbitrating claims to validity; if knowledge is 'useful' or 'practically adequate' then somehow whether it is true or false, correct or incorrect is neither here nor there. This, of course, is totally antithetical to the position that I have outlined so far in this book since I have argued that any form of knowledge including 'practical adequacy' itself (in whatever guise, and there must be many) is underpinned by epistemological claims.

To seize on 'practical adequacy' as the linchpin of validity claims in realism would be to sever realism from claims to cognitive adequacy which both positivism and humanism uphold. Thus, this would be to cede the whole terrain of truth claims to realism's main competitors! The problem with practical adequacy as a primitive concept is that it has no boundaries and a weak discriminatory propensity. Thus, many things can be admitted as valid or adequate knowledge simply because they 'work' in particular contexts. As I said before, if we restrict the notion to the physical world it may appear to be a *more* reasonable assumption to make; thus water does not provide us with a stable surface to walk on. However, of course, the social world has very little to do with problems such as whether we can walk on water. Western civilisation and the knowledge that it has produced has not been limited by this fact, hence we have produced boats, bridges, aircraft which have obviated the problem! When we discuss practical adequacy in a social context we have to ask questions such as practically adequate for what, and for whom! And if we do so we quickly move out of any realm of 'innocence' that might have been presumed by a concentration on the natural world. For instance, the arguments, symbols and ideology which passed for knowledge in Nazi Germany and which led to the holocaust were 'practically adequate' to the Nazis in their effort to murder Europe's Jews, but surely no-one would argue that this practical adequacy undergirded and legitimated the validity or the *truth* of Nazi ideas about extermination, purification, and the like. Such 'knowledge' is judged by quite other means than practical adequacy. (Moreover, insofar as this forced them to divert scarce resources from vital military aims, it was not in the long-term even practically adequate.)

Similarly, different kinds of social theoretical knowledge which generate descriptions of social reality in terms of functional inter-dependencies, class antagonisms, the indexicality of members accounts cannot be simply judged in terms of their practical utility. Such an approach would lead to a practical (or practitioner-defined) relativism of social knowledge (a parallel to the cognitive relativism produced in the conventionalist account). Certainly, the whole edifice of functionism is practically adequate for functionalists, as is ethnomethodology for ethnomethodologists, and Marxism for Marxists. There can be no sensible adjudication of validity claims based on practical adequacy; there has to be some invocation of cognitive adequacy and explanatory power, based ultimately on various truth and validity claims and defined in terms of critical departure from both earlier and extant competing theories.

Those who advocate practical adequacy seem to envisage this as the only alternative to positivist strict correspondence or conventionalist relativism in which virtually any reasoned claim to validity is deemed adequate. In this manner practical adequacy is proposed not as an alternative truth claim but an alternative to truth claims in general. This leads as I have said to an unprincipled practical relativism especially in relation to social knowledge and a disavowal of the notions of principled and discriminatory criteria of cognitive adequacy. For realism to compete successfully with positivism and humanism it must not abandon the quest for cognitive adequacy and the pursuance of truth claims about the adequacy of representations of the objects of knowledge.

As I said before, this requires realism to adopt an alternative notion of truth to the conventionalist and the positivist 'correspondence' versions, not to abandon the pursuit altogether. The most appropriate strategy in this respect would be to adopt some middle ground between correspondence and coherence theories of truth.

That is, to sustain the notion of reference to external objects of knowledge which is implicit in the notion of correspondence, *without* endorsing the idea that the relationship between concepts (internal referents) and objects of knowledge (external referents) is *isomorphic*. Similarly, whilst endorsing the coherence notion that the meaning of a concept within a theory or conceptual network is to some extent dependent on its interrelations with the other concepts in the network, we must avoid the implication that objects of knowledge are only constituted within discourse and have no operational existence independent of our cognising experience (as in Althusserian formulations. Althusser 1969; Hindess and Hirst 1977).

Such middle ground would preserve the idea of a world of real structures and generative mechanisms independent of cognising experience, but would sustain two other notions. First, that whilst knowledge and the world are ontologically and analytically independent of each other, we *can only know the world* through linguistic and conceptional representations of that world. That is, knowledge of the world is given in, or takes the form of, already constructed knowledge in the shape of conceptual and theoretical instruments and epistemological premises. Second, such middle ground would sustain the idea that knowledge attempts to *represent* objects which are, to varying degrees, independent of its discursive parameters. Of course, it must be remembered here that this representation is a symbolic representation; it is not an appropriation of or isomorphic depiction of these objects. Such a theory of truth might usefully be termed a concomitance theory of truth.

ONTOLOGY AND TRUTH CLAIMS

Bhaskar's (1979) attempt to construct a realist naturalism displays little concern with the problems (or nature of) theorising in sociology or social psychology in terms of the discursive parameters I have outlined and thus also little concern with the criteria of validity that can be applied to realist knowledge. Despite some claims to have 'resolved' the conflicting insights of empiricism and rationalism, Bhaskar's work displays a latent empiricism as a result of a concern with the privileged nature of ontology, as against the privileged nature of observation and experience that the realists impute to positivist methods. It is precisely this change of emphasis that convinces realists that they have circumnavigated the problem of empiri-

cism. Instead of concentrating upon experience and observational
methods, the realist concentrates upon the real (but not necessarily
observable) structures of the world, which are the objects of our
scientific knowledge, and which in fact determine our knowledge of
them. Thus, Bhaskar states that,

> For transcendental realism, it is the nature of objects that deter-
> mines their cognitive possibilities for us . . . in nature it is man
> that is contingent and knowledge, so to speak, accidental. Thus it
> is because sticks and stones are solid that they can be picked up
> and thrown, not because they can be picked up and thrown that
> they are solid! . . . (1979, p. 31)

It is not that there is not a grain of truth in Bhaskar's formulation
but rather that it constructs arbitrary parameters on the determination of knowledge. These parameters are essentially empiricist
ones, in so far as empiricism is used to cover cases where there is a
denial of the influence of rational discourse in the determination of
knowledge. This rational determination is denied in the sense that
it is 'the nature of objects that determines their cognitive possibilities
for us'. In this manner Bhaskar believes that he has bypassed the
empiricism implicit in the positivist faith in the use of experimental
and observational techniques as the ultimate guarantors of truth.
However, he has done this by utilising an even more primitive term
– 'ontology' (the given real nature of the object world) – which, in
this scheme is prior to and independent of, both observation and
experience and our scientific knowledge (of the things referred to by
the term ontology). Instead of our knowledge being given to us
through our observations (traditional empiricism), it is given to us
by the prior structures of the world which constitute an irreducible
reality (the 'intransitive dimension of science') and thus act as determinate limits on our knowledge. Since Bhaskar is more concerned
with describing what the ontological features of society actually are
(I deal with these below), the question of how knowledge is produced
in this way is never fully explicated by him and thus remains at the
level of implicit claims rather than systematic demonstration. More
generally, Bhaskar omits consideration of the nature of the relationship between scientific theories and the objects which they describe,
and the status and properties of theory (in general) and theoretical
discourse in particular.

If we take up the analogy that Bhaskar himself uses we can see
immediately the errors in this kind of argument. For Bhaskar, the

fact that 'sticks and stones are solid', determines our knowledge 'that they can be picked up and thrown'; I would want to agree with this statement up to a point, but disagree with the implication that this is the whole of the story. I would argue that it is possible to speak of the recalcitrant or obdurate character of some (particularly physical) ontological features in the very limited sense that they may constrain particular aspects of our knowledge. For example, there may be a link, say, between the hardness of stones and certain forms of practical knowledge and/or uses, such as the throwability of stones, or the building of walls, but this is only one aspect of our knowledge of stones, since they are not exclusively involved in such narrowly conceived practical activities. For instance, 'stones' may be revered as sacred objects themselves, or as symbolic representations in mystical or religious rites (Stonehenge); they may be collected by archaeologists as examples of stone weapons and geologists as scientific data, or by collectors as cultural or aesthetic objects, or by sculptors as raw material out of which an artistic form may emerge. Such knowledge of stones is not given to us by an examination of their ontological (physical) features, such as solidity; in these cases they are what they are, namely, aesthetic or sacred objects, scientific data and the like not because of some transcendentally real nature, but rather because they have a determinate place in a specific scheme of knowledge.

Moving away from the stones analogy, the same is true of the social world, in so far as it is a mistake to think that we can deduce a veridical epistemology from an uncontaminated (pre-theoretical) examination of the ontological structure of the world. Moreover, such an assumption is the result of an empiricist epistemological premise, that is, that the natural and eternal structures of reality reveal an immanent truth. The point is that knowledge of the social world is not solely given by some immanent and transcendent 'reality' (ontological features in Bhaskar's terms), but by the way or ways in which it is known. Thus, Bhaskar does not see the relativity and partiality of the claims he makes about the ontological limits of naturalism in social science in relation to other possible claims. The ontological limits that Bhaskar identifies are threefold. First, Bhaskar claims that unlike natural structures, social structures do not exist independently of the activities they govern. Second, unlike natural structures, social structures do not exist independently of the agents' conceptions of what they are doing in their activity. Third, and again unlike natural structures, social structures may be only relatively enduring. For present purposes the contrast between the natural and social sciences does not concern us, although Benton (1981) has recently challenged Bhaskar's claims. Similarly, the third claim about the relatively enduring character of social structures does not presently concern us.

The question that needs to be raised in relation to the first two ontological limits, namely, the concept and activity dependence of social structures is whether and in what sense they are true? I would argue that the idea that social structures do not exist independently of the activities they govern and the agents' conceptions of what they are doing is only true within the terms of an exclusively empiricist epistemology and thus an individualist/voluntarist conception of social structure (despite Bhaskar's claim to the contrary). There are a number of closely associated and highly complicated issues which surround the problematic concept of structure, many of which cannot be fully entered into here for reasons of space. Not the least of these complications is, exactly what is meant by a *social structure?* The further question of whether all social structures are of the same form is equally pivotal to the establishment of Bhaskar's claim to have described the true and irreducible ontological features that societies possess.

However, in general terms it can be seen that from the perspective of a rationalist/structuralist epistemological position (for instance, the discourses of scientific Marxism and structuralism) the very existence of enduring social relations presupposes at the very least a *relative independence* or relative autonomy of such structures. That is, without reifying social structures by insisting that they exist and operate independently of human activity or human intervention *altogether*, there are at least two senses in which social structures are not activity or concept dependent. The first is the sense in which enduring social relations (that is, social structures), exist and are reproduced over time independently of the activities and conceptions of specific individuals or specific groups of individuals who are subject to them. For example, the social structure of capitalism, although dependent upon wage labour or workers *in general* to ensure its reproduction, is not dependent upon specific workers or specific groups of workers (for example, particular firms or even sometimes particular kinds of industry) for its survival.

The second sense in which social structures are not dependent on the activities of agents relates to the properties and functioning of structures at particular points in time. Benton (1981) points to the ambiguities and insufficiencies of Bhaskar's formulation by taking the example of power structure:

> The concept of a power-structure required in empirical sociological research must enable the investigator to identify power-relations where powers are not, in fact, exercised though they continue to be possessed. In such cases, the activities constituting the exercise of powers (governed by the power structure?) are not necessary to the existence of the power structure (though other activities may well be). The full coercive power of the state, for example, may continue to be possessed without being exercised, though such activities as the raising of taxes, the recruiting, training and equipping of armed personnel may well be necessary to the maintenance of that structure of power relations. (1981, p. 17.)

The purpose of this excursus on the nature of social structures has been to fill out the earlier more general argument against Bhaskar's claim about the priority of ontology (see also, examples given in following section). Thus, as with the previous analogy about the nature of stones and their uses, I have tried to demonstrate here that an ontology of the social can never be an uncontestable and transcendentally given thing; it is always as it were, 'overdetermined' by a theoretical discourse and an epistemology. That is, the differing epistemological premises of different theoretical discourses produce different and sometimes competing versions of a social ontology and hence, competing conceptions of the nature of social structures. Thus, the empiricism of Bhaskar's formulations is resonated in two ways. First, by according a privileged priority to ontology Bhaskar is implicitly claiming there is an extra-theoretical givenness to the structures of reality which, as a result, determines our knowledge of them. Second, the empiricism of this method has led Bhaskar to an empiricist (and thus arbitrarily limited), conception of social structure as activity- and concept-dependent. Thus, it could be said that whilst Keat and Urry are rather more concerned with the criteria of validity of realist knowledge than is Bhaskar, who is more concerned with identifying the real structures themselves in terms of a transcendental argument, their mutual (sophisticated) empiricism derives from a similar source; the privileged but unargued role they accord to ontology in the determination of knowledge.

Giddens (1984), albeit in a rather different context, also argues for the priority of ontological matters. He implies that a preoccupation with epistemological issues, such as verification or falsification, represents a diversion from more pressing concerns of an ontological nature, such as 'reworking conceptions of human being and human doing' (p. xx). The 'key problems' of social analysis are intrinsically ontological in nature rather than epistemological, because they are concerned in an immediate sense with the way in which social reality in constituted. Giddens is right that an exclusive preoccupation with epistemological matters would represent something of a barrier to the advancement of social analysis, especially with regard to reworking conceptions of human being and human doing and the like. However, Giddens is wrong to imply that his own analysis, preoccupied as it is with ontological concerns, is somehow free of problems of verification and validity.

Giddens' here comes close to an assertion of the self-validation of his own position. This results from his wholehearted endorsement of an exclusively humanist (or existential-phenomenological) conception of ontology. In this conception the category of ontology refers to a notion of social reality as constituted precisely by those things that Giddens takes to be essential, namely, human being and doing. This conception automatically cuts out of purview any notion of social reality as being also constituted, in part, by impersonal 'external' or 'objective' social forces or properties, which constitute a relatively independent domain (see Popper 1972). However, this filtering out of alternative conceptions is not explicitly argued for or defended; it is simply and silently imported as a basic premise of the argument disguised by the supposedly self-evident (and exhaustive) ingredients of ontology; that is, human doing and being.

Indeed, the whole question of the conceptuality of characterisations of ontology (and therefore the social theoretical conditions that govern their production) can never be raised if ontology is already defined in terms of a specific conceptual appropriation of a given or self-evident reality. Analysis is begun from premises that masquerade as self-evident truths rather than from inherently contestable claims about how we 'know' reality. The question of what we take to be the basic features of social reality is inseparable from questions relating to the procedures we adopt in coming to know this reality.

The unargued assertion of a specific conception of social ontology thus secures, at the same time as it conceals, a definite link with an empiricist theory of knowledge, a link that Giddens would otherwise be keen to deny (p. xvi). The empiricism of Giddens' position here is unlike the usual form of empiricism wherein the 'experience' of an observer or analyst is taken to be a passive register of events in the world. Its very formulation fails to acknowledge its own theoretical construction as one possibility among others. The empiricism is reflected in the way Giddens portrays ontology as a characterisation of the social world that is isomorphic with that world, rather than a theoretically underpinned interpretation of the world (Layder 1985b).

Epistemologically, this move is a necessary precondition of Giddens' (later) rejection of objectivism because it allows him to say that social reality is coextensive with the active subjects who produce social activity and cannot be understood in any external, objective sense. Thus, an empiricist strategy that accepts the social world as self-evidently constituted by nothing more and nothing less than the 'doing and being' of active, skilled human subjects is already an unargued rejection of an objectivist ontology.

This empiricist residuum is also a denial of the hermeneutic starting point upon which Giddens otherwise so strenuously insists. The assertion of the priority of ontological matters in general, and of one conception in particular, is tantamount to suggesting that the basic features of social reality are not subject to the normal 'mediation of frames of meaning', which in this case are primarily theoretical. In short, it does not appear that they form part of the 'double hermeneutic' that figures so prominently in Giddens' work (1976, 1979).

CONCLUSION

At the beginning of this chapter I outlined some aspects of the debate between rationalism and empiricism which bear upon the general question of truth claims in social science. I suggested that one way in which competing claims to scientific truth could be evaluated was in terms of the degree to which any truth claim resolved the twin restriction problems of empiricism and extreme rationalism. In subsequent sections I have sought to show that in various ways realism has failed to transcend the restrictions of empiricism by failing to incorporate some appreciation of the role of the rational properties of discourse. In particular, realism has consistently undertheorised the way in which the linguistically mediated cognitive and perceptual effects of theoretical discourses have a predispositional role in the constituting of the objects of discourse. My argument has been that realism should attend to these generative mechanisms of discourse (as they would any other generative mechanisms), without relinquishing the idea of an operationally independent of object world.

In the context of such a modified realist approach to truth claims I have examined three aspects of realist validity claims. The first concerned the role of observation in the falsification or validation of theoretical entities. I argued that despite the formal realist insistence on the theory-laden character of observation there is a tendency for realists to overlook the detailed implications of this view in attempting to set up validational criteria using observational means.

Second, I examined the specific proposal that the notion of truth should be substituted by the notion of practical adequacy. I rejected this idea on the grounds that it leads to a pragmatic relativism. To the contrary, I argued that a necessary feature of the realist project must be to uphold the notion of cognitive adequacy.

Finally, I took a very critical view of the idea that ontological features are privileged and that they are somehow more important than epistemological issues. In particular, I rejected the view that it is the nature of the objects of knowledge that determines their cognitive possibilities for us. Such a view is ensnared by the limitations imposed by an empiricist view of the nature and origins of knowledge and does not square with realist claims in two senses. First, it arbitrarily narrows the scope of knowledge by reproducing and reaffirming the empiricist restrictions I outlined earlier, and second, it is directly contrary to the formal claim that realism has transcended the problem of empiricism.

4 Causality, Acausality and the Implicate Order

In chapters 2 and 3 I have concentrated primarily on the epistemological context of realist knowledge claims. That is, I have dealt with such things as the origins, the scope, the nature and validity of knowledge produced under the auspices of realism. In this chapter, I want to begin to address some primarily ontological issues. In chapter 1 I suggested that the realist model (or models) of social ontology unnecessarily constricts the domain of legitimate explanation in the social sciences and as a consequence, narrows its explanatory scope. In chapter 5 I shall argue more generally for an extension of the model of social ontology and outline some specific recommendations. Here I shall concentrate on one particular ontological feature which does not appear in the realist scheme of things; that is, the notion of an implicate order.

To begin to approach this issue, however, we must go back to the question of causality in realism. In a sense, the issue of causality can be seen to be, and treated as, both part of the explanatory (epistemological) context of social science, as well as a feature of the object or ontological context. How can this be so? Perhaps the relation of causality to the explanatory context is more apparent since this represents the orthodox view. In this sense particular phenomena of the social world are understood to bear necessary and/or contingent relations with one another. It is this presupposition which confers on social science the possibility of a *depth* dimension to analysis. For if it is the case that certain phenomena do bear these kinds of reciprocally influential relationships then it seems plausible that explanation of such phenomena may be couched in terms of the dynamics and mechanics of these relationships, rather than *simply* in terms of the description and classification of the phenomena themselves.

That is, social science is thus free to go beyond the description and classification of the phenomena of social reality and to posit explanatory accounts of how they have come into existence, what sort of effects they produce in related phenomena, and why concatenations or configurations of phenomena exhibit the specific patterns they do exhibit. In the positivist account of science the Humean

conception of causality attempted to represent this kind of explanation, albeit in a fairly minimalistic fashion. Thus, the search was
begun for the patterned regularities in the observed relations
between phenomena. In this tradition the notion of a cause was
thought to be an external antecedent event which impinges on
another event and produces this event as a causal effect. Causal laws
are thus said to express the constant conjuncture of externally related
events or states (Wilson 1982).

Realism suggests that this kind of causal 'explanation' does not
sufficiently depart from a descriptive depiction of observed states of
affairs in the guise of constant conjunctions. A truly explanatory
causal explanation would want to go beyond the description of manifest regularities and attempt to account for these regularities by
reference to the real underlying structures that produce these
manifestations.

The realist alternative or 'generative theory' suggests that cause
and effect are not discrete phenomena; they are internally related in
the sense that causes are seen to be mechanisms which possess the
power to produce effects when stimulated. This idea does not deny
that empirical regularities occur in the world, but does deny that the
laws expressing constant conjunctions are sufficient to explain these
regularities. Rather, attention is focussed on the reasons for the
existence of the regularity itself and this is explained in terms of
'natural necessity'. In this formulation

> A thing comes to do something by virtue of its having a certain
> constitution or structure. A sharp distinction is therefore drawn
> between the idea of cause as an antecedent event which triggers
> a mechanism and the mechanism itself. For example, the molecular
> structure of glass makes it brittle, such that, if it is hit by a flying
> rock, it will break. The rock 'causes' the glass to break, but the
> molecular structure is actually the mechanism whereby the out-
> come is achieved. Discovering this mechanism (rather than the
> rock) explains the breaking of glass.
>
> (Wilson 1982, pp. 251–2)

Now I would not want to disagree with the general realist argument
here, namely, that we should be searching for generatively causal
mechanisms as opposed to describing correlationally causal 'events'.
I believe, however, that fundamental disagreements ensue from subsequent attempts to characterise particular generative mechanisms
in the social world as the 'basic' or 'dominant' mechanisms. Alterna-

tively, it would be an issue of contention whether certain social phenomena have causal status conferred upon them, or conversely whether they are denied such status. Such issues will feature in the discussion in the next chapter, where I deal with the question of ontology.

This brings me to the second area of contention in relation to the concept of causality and returns our attention to the question of the different senses in which causality can be understood as epistemological or ontological. The search for causal mechanisms and causal phenomena in general calls attention to a specific class of social phenomena by reason of their causal relevance (that is, they are either the causal mechanisms themselves, or they are in some sense *informative* about causality). In this sense the analytical concentration on causal mechanisms has the effect of displacing (if not wholly precluding) a concern with phenomena which have no obvious connection with causal mechanisms nor *seem* to be in any way informative about causal relations. Thus, in this sense the concern with causality etches in the contours of ontological reference and relevance and thus tends to ignore the explanatory importance of acausal phenomena.

I believe it is important for realism to be able to incorporate a concern with acausal phenomena, since to ignore them would be to restrict the explanatory scope of realism in an entirely arbitrary way. In this sense the skewing of analytic concern towards causal phenomena is analogically related to egocentrism or ethnocentrism where there is an inability either to see beyond, or see the relevance of, what lies beyond the familiar and linguistically habituated centre of attention. Such a call for the decentring of causality is not a call for the dissipation of the power of analytic focus by spreading the notion of explanatory relevance in an even and relativistic way. This is where a distinction between acausal and general non-causal phenomena becomes important.

I want to distinguish between general non-causal phenomena which have no particular explanatory status (other than perhaps being some minor segment of a specific phenomenon being studied) and genuinely *A*causal phenomena which can be regarded as generative loci. They are acausal because they are generative in a different sense from the causal mechanisms of realism. I do not want so much to draw a stark contrast between the modes of operation of causal and acausal phenomena, but rather to get away from the 'mechanistic' linear-chain metaphor which attends the question of causality in both its positivist and realist guises.

In this sense I conceive of acausal phenomena in a way which does not tie them to the identification of mechanisms which represent specific causal sites and which produce specific effects when the mechanism is stimulated. By contrast, acausal phenomena represent the relation between discrete phenomena and the reciprocally influential effects that result from these interdependencies. In this way, acausal phenomena are not located *within* specific chains of causes and effects even if these causes and effects are understood to be internally related. Rather, acausal phenomena should be understood as possessing powers which exert diffuse influences and produce diffuse effects by virtue of the internal structures of phenomena, and as a consequence of their interaction with each other. The mode in which these diffuse influences and effects present themselves has to be understood as continuous and even, rather than discrete and punctuated in the manner of linear sequences of latency-stimulation-causal effects-latency-stimulation and so on (see Figure 4.3, p. 95).

In the analysis which follows this introduction I attempt to show how the idea-world of social science (epistemological, theoretical and methodological discourses) represents an implicate order of acausal phenomena which influences our understanding of the relationship between theory and method in sociology in particular, and social science in general. This example will also illustrate a further feature of acausal phenomena; their intimate relationship with the world of causality. In this sense an acausal analysis adds to a causal account and is informative in an explanatory sense but not in a causal sense.

Thus, the following analysis will attempt to illustrate how the explicate order of causality and practice in social science is acausally influenced by the implicate order. The relationship between the explicate order (the causal, experiential world) and the implicate order (acausal interdependencies between ideas or conceptual networks) has to be expressed in acausal terms since the explicate order tends to preclude the explanatory import of the implicate order in the first place. The following analysis is structured around a critical dialogue with ideas set forward by Jennifer Platt in an article which discusses the general relationship between theory and method in sociology as a result of a specific examination of functionalism and survey research in post-war US society. In the context of my preceding comments on the importance of acausal phenomena for realism my discussion questions the extent to which Platt's analysis and general conclusions mask important levels of connectedness between theory and method.

After this discussion of the general relation of theory and method as an example of the usefulness of the notions of acausality and the implicate and explicate orders, the second half of this chapter focusses on the notion of causality itself as realists have appropriated it from naturalism. To put it another way, it focusses on the way in which realists have rescued the notion of causality from the limitations imposed on it by positivism. I want to defend the realist version from misplaced criticisms which follow from a prior misrepresentation of its explanatory role in natural science.

The final part of the chapter takes a detailed look at the realist version of causality and asks whether its terms of reference also, can be usefully broadened out. In this respect I ask whether the realist version of causality has freed itself totally from the restrictions of the positivist account. I suggest that the realist version is still influenced to some degree by the metaphor of a linear-chain, which is deeply embedded in the positivist version. As a consequence of this, I sketch a preliminary model of a mosaic (or network) conception of generative loci. This model represents an attempt to preserve the advantages that the realist account has over the positivist account, whilst broadening its scope and reducing its dependence upon the linear-chain metaphor. My discussion of this issue ends on a deliberately ambiguous note, and expresses itself in the form of a question. If the very notion of causality is so deeply imbued with the linear-chain image, does realism need to abandon the linguistic label (of 'causality') whilst retaining of course, its interest in generative phenomena which constitute its main focus of interest and one of its most distinctive features?

THE RELATION OF THEORY AND METHOD

Before discussing the idea of causality by using Platt's (1986) ideas as a vehicle for developing my own, let me enter a few cautionary caveats about my intentions, since a cursory reading may produce quite serious misunderstandings and misrepresentations (see Platt 1988 and Bulmer 1988, and the discussion in the Appendix). I think that those who have read the previous chapters carefully will not be prone to these kinds of errors, but nonetheless let me be absolutely unequivocal from the start. What follows is neither a denial of the usefulness of empirical research, nor a confusion (and thus, a conflation) of history with philosophy. As to the question of empirical research in general I think I have indicated already that my interest is in the question of *how* to characterise the relationship between theory and evidence (the internal and external referents of discourse) and not to deny the relevance of one at the expense of the other. (This, in fact, is the upshot of my discussion of the empiricist-rationalist debate.)

The idea that I am treating philosophy as though it were history is a variant of the accusation that I deny the relevance of the empirical world of research, and is just as unfounded. Clearly, I do not take philosophy or history to be the same thing (or about the same things); nonetheless I do take epistemological questions (to be more precise) to be indispensable to the understanding of the relationship between theory and method even if this relationship is presented as an historical account. This is the focus of my discussion of Platt's work. Basically, I take issue with her argument that historical accounts of the relation of theory and method can be adjudicated solely in historical or empirical terms.

My argument is that epistemological and historical issues can and must be seen as complementary, although I do not see this relation as a simple one. In this sense I am against the *privileging* of historical or empirical material with regard to the question of the general relation between theory and method. In the light of these comments I hope it will be appreciated that I am attempting to tease out the ramifications of what is now something of a sociological truism – that empirical inquiry (history, observation, data) is theory-laden. Of course, and most importantly, I am using the term 'theory' here in a multi-dimensional sense which attempts to capture the underlying *presuppositions* of different kinds of social scientific discourse. In particular, I stress the importance of basic knowledge premises and how these affect and relate to the more ontological components of theory and practice in social science.

Platt (1986) questions some recent assumptions that have been made about the general relationship between sociological theories and methods. She does this in the context of a detailed examination of the extent to which functionalist theory and survey method were in practice related in post-war US sociology. By a historical 'reconstruction' of what actually happened, aided by data from interviews with some of the practitioners involved, Platt convincingly demonstrates that there was no causal connection between functionalism and survey method, in the sense that the latter was dependent on the former.

From her empirical analysis Platt concludes that 'in so far as functionalism and the survey were dominant at the same time, the relationship between them is more like a merely ecological correlation than a causal connection' (p. 527). She is careful to point out that more generally she is not arguing that 'theory and method are *never* causally related, or have special one-to-one intellectual affinities'. She suggests, for instance, that in this respect a more convincing case can be made about the relation between symbolic interactionism and participant observation, than functionalism and survey methods (p. 528–9). Rather, she is arguing that theory and method have no *necessary* causal relationship, and 'that in practice research methods have more autonomy than the account criticised implies' (p. 529). In her final sentence she summarises what is a constant motif of her paper; the distinction between what *is* the case and what *ought* to be the case.

> The tendency to see theory and method as intimately related has in it, both in this case and more generally, more of ideology about what the relation ought to be than it has of close historical observation of what actually happened. (p. 530)

Now while I do feel that Platt has successfully demonstrated her case about the relation between functionalism and the survey along a number of historically documented dimensions such as whether functionalism was prior to the survey, whether functionalists preferred surveys, whether survey researchers were functionalists and so on, her analysis also raises a number of questions which are not tackled in her paper. Since Platt is making general points about the relation between theory and method it seems important to pinpoint these issues.

My primary objective here is to attempt to broaden out the terms of the discussion of the *general relation* between theory and method as it is portrayed in Platt's paper. That is, I believe that Platt's treatment unnecessarily constricts the terms of the discussion in two ways. First, by derogating the importance of what I would call the 'rational connections' between theories and methods as compared with causal and/or empirically contingent connections. Second, by insisting on the intrinsic separateness of epistemological and historical or empirical questions Platt's analysis ignores their reciprocal effects. Most importantly, in relation to the previous point, since historical/empirical analysis is construed as autonomous, the effects of epistemological concerns (particularly as evidenced by rational connections) on actual research practice are obscured.

These constrictions tend to reinforce one another in Platt's analysis. Against this, I want to argue that epistemological and empirical questions are intrinsically entangled and that some account of the implications of this can be an important source of illumination in the research and analysis of the relation between theory and method. Although Platt's approach is valid and significant as *a level* of analysis in its own right, in so far as it is seen as in some way 'privileged' or implying the constrictions mentioned above, then my intention is to question these assumptions and to emphasise once more the importance of what are basically philosophical issues.

It must be said from the beginning that some, but not all, of the difference between my own and Platt's views stem from a difference in use of the term 'theory'. Some of my reservations about the more universalising aspects of Platt's thesis centre on her decision to define 'theories' as those which are 'commonly recognized and named within the discipline' (p. 504 – presumably of sociology). It is clear, from her article as a whole that what she means by 'theories' are, otherwise termed, 'schools of theory' such as functionalism, Marxism, symbolic interactionism and the like. This narrow definition of theory is important to remember when it comes to an assessment of Platt's views on the *general* relationship between theory and method (as opposed to the specific relationship between functionalism and the survey). In this sense, when Platt moves from the particular to the general she still retains the narrow definition of theory (as 'schools' of social theory). This narrowing of the notion of theory in itself, has the effect of narrowing the band of *possible* relations between theory and method.

In this respect I would argue that when speaking of the relation between theory and method *in general terms* it is more meaningful to unpack the variant meanings of the term 'theory' in order that we may expose and identify the different levels of theoretical *presuppositions* that bear some relation to research methods. There are four types of theoretical presupposition that are involved here. First, and most basic, are epistemological presuppositions (ranging along the continuum between empiricism and rationalism) which underpin any form of knowledge. The second concerns the specific model of social science which undergirds particular sociological propositions (positivism, humanism and realism). Third, there are social theoretical discourses, or 'schools of theory' for example, functionalism, symbolic interactionism and so on, that is, what Platt terms 'theory'. Fourth, there are methodological presuppositions which specify in advance the form that theory should take as it emerges from the research process. This I shall term 'research theory', and 'middle-range theory' and 'grounded-theory' are examples of this.

I shall elaborate on these different types of theoretical presupposition in due course; it simply needs to be pointed out here that if one admits these variant meanings of theoretical presuppositions to the definition of 'theory', then this in itself widens the scope of possible statements one can make about the relations between theory and method. Similarly, if one takes into account the whole range of theoretical presuppositions then it is also clear that 'method' itself can never be completely severed from such presuppositions. Thus, whilst a specific method such as survey research may not be paired exclusively with any school of theory, methods in general are, none-theless, underpinned by specific epistemological assumptions includ-ing a specific conception of social science (in the case of the survey positivism). It must be noted here that by pointing to epistemological and ontological features of theory and theorising I am *not* suggesting (as has been alleged) that this somehow leads to a 'relativising of standpoints' and merely adds to 'the confusion which afflicts British sociology'. Indeed, if shedding light on, and understanding the differ-ent kinds of premises which underpin theory and theorising are deemed to be obfuscations of the sociological enterprise then this in itself is one of the most depressing sources of confusion which afflicts some (aggressively insular) sociological standpoints. Far from pro-posing a *complete* relativism, I am pointing to a highly specific and limited relativism which derives from implicit commitments and attachments to the deep-rooted assumptions which underlie theory and method.

Platt seems to envisage three distinct possibilities for the relation between theory and method. The first posits a *necessary* causal con-nection between theory and method such that the former determines the latter in some way. This account is 'normative not empirical' (p. 506) and whilst Platt is not *in principle* absolutely against the norma-tive, she is extremely concerned to undermine accounts which *con-fuse* the normative with the empirical. Thus, taken as an *a priori* truth, the necessary causation account *does* make this confusion, and indeed, the whole point of her empirical analysis of the relation between functionalism and the survey method is geared to exposing the distortions of truth which occur when the normative takes precedence over the empirical, in what are basically empirical/historical questions.

The second possible version of the relation between theory and method, and the one she utilises in her historical/empirical reconstruction of the relation between functionalism and the survey, is much looser in form and is entirely dependent on the historical uncovering of the empirical truth of the matter. Thuss, in this account one would expect the relation between theory and method to be a much less neat one emphasising the relative autonomy of practice (method) and the historically contingent nature of the tie. This, of course, does not entirely rule out the possibility of causal relatedness, but nonetheless makes this very causal relatedness the outcome of historical contingency rather than the result of a necessary and intrinsic feature of the relationship between theory and method. The third possibility that Platt envisages concern relations of 'mere' affinity or 'compatibility' between various theories and methods. These are 'mere' in the sense that they are 'uninformative about causation – *empirical historical* causation in particular cases'.

It is in relation to the third version that Platt understands the domain of epistemological matters. However, before moving on to the substance of Platt's paper I want decisively to reject the imputation that this area is of minor importance with regard to the relation between theory and method. I also want to reject the associated idea that the importance of what I would prefer to term 'rational connections' can be arbitrated in terms of whether or not they are 'informative about causation'.

THE IMPLICATE AND EXPLICATE ORDERS

Let me sketch out, therefore, what I would take to be an alternative to Platt's notion of 'mere affinities' or compatibilities. In this sense I am agreeing with Platt's first two possibilities, the notion of necessary causation and the notion of historical contingency, but I am disagreeing with the idea that the importance of epistemological questions and rational connections should be derogated by being characterised in a way which both prejudges the issue (the derogatory 'mere') and assumes that which needs to be demonstrated, namely, that such connections are in some way *weaker* than, and thus inherently subordinate to, causal connections.

Also, let it be clear that, with Platt, I would want to reject the pure idea of necessary causal relatedness, not because in many cases it does not stand the test of empirical evidence, but more importantly because it is not a helpful way of characterising lines of mutual influence between knowledge premises and the methods that social analysts use in empirical research. (This is not to question Platt's assertion that some authors have indeed offered the causal related-ness account as the defining characteristic of the relationship between theory and method.) We may also agree that in the specific case of functionalism and the survey the historical contingency account is superior to the necessary causality account in that it provides a decisive 'testing out' of the causality account. But I do want to reject the *general* imputation that the relation between theory and method should be primarily characterised in terms of a test of a causal hypothesis. At the same time I want to reject the concomitant idea that the only other relations between theory and method are 'mere affinities' or 'compatibilities' which are insignificant because they are uninformative about causation.

Now, what are these rational connections between different levels of theory and method? First, they concern the link between bodies of ideas forming clusterings of theoretical presuppositions, and par-ticular kinds of research practice. The underlying assumption is that research practice (method) is never 'autonomous' with regard to such bodies of ideas. Whether in general or in particular manifestations, practice always occurs in the context of environing bodies of ideas and bears some reciprocally influential relationship to them (regard-less of whether particular practitioners are aware of these ideas and their influence – see later comments.) These bodies of ideas are clearly named and defined within both the psychological and social sciences and philosophy, and examples are 'empiricism', 'rational-ism', 'positivism', 'humanism', 'realism', 'functionalism', 'symbolic interactionism' and the like.

Now, the links between such bodies of ideas and research practices which the phrase 'rational connections' points to have nothing to do with causality either in its Humean guise, as constant conjunctions of events conceived of in linear sequential terms (Platt's conception) or in its realist guise as the relation between underlying generative mechanisms which give rise to observable phenomena. I would characterise the link as one of *acausal interdependence* between two orders of social reality: the idea-world and the world of practice.

I think that Bohm's (1981) characterisation of an implicate and explicate order in relation to the physical universe is an evocative way of describing these two orders of social reality. In this sense the implicate order refers to the objective world of ideas (a 'third world' in Popper's terms) from which defined bodies of ideas, or more accurately, clusterings of (related) concepts emerge as social constructions in time and space. A crucial feature of the idea-world is that it possesses an objective content (also a crucial aspect of Popper's 1971 notion of a 'third world') which is generated by its social reproduction over time and space. As such, this objective content confers upon the idea-world a relative independence from the ongoing flux of everyday social practices in general, and research practices in particular.

The explicate order in fact refers to this latter world of lived, experienced, human practice. It is this explicate order which is constantly emphasised in Western thought and language and, indeed, is the basis of the traditional scientific (Humean) notion of causality based on observed regularities of successions of pairs of events. By contrast, the implicate order is not emphasised in the habitual thought world fashioned by our linguistic tools, geared as they are to signalling the overt, observable and sequential (Bohm 1981). As a direct consequence of this, the *relationship* between the two orders has to be understood as itself part of the implicate order, and is therefore not *accessible* to, or through, the explicate order of sequential causality to which we have become cognitively and perceptually habituated.

On the basis of what I have already said, I would reject the imputation that I am interested in bodies of ideas 'in themselves' as if they could be *ultimately* divorced from practice. However, to say this is not to say that bodies of ideas cannot be examined independently of specific instances of practice, nor that in themselves they have no partly independent properties. These latter in fact represent an equally important aspect of my concerns since, if it is the case that defined bodies of ideas with their own partly independent properties do exist, then understanding what these latter are becomes a necessary precondition for understanding their relation to practice.

There are three aspects to these partly autonomous properties. First, as I have already mentioned, ideas in themselves have an objective non-reified existence in general. More germane to present concerns is the second aspect, which focusses on subsets of idea-clusters; bodies of ideas which are named and defined in the disciplines I mentioned previously. Thus, such idea-clusters as 'empiricism', 'rationalism' 'positivism' and so on can be understood and analysed internally as relatively integrated networks (or clusterings) of concepts. Even more important than the internal structure of such clusterings are the relationships *between* particular networks. The notion of 'rational connections' rests upon the idea that certain conceptual networks share some portion of their conceptual and cognitive content, as well as their scope and domain of relevance.

Thus, for example, empiricism (and its different varieties) represents a theory of knowledge at its most basic and fundamental level which underpins and thus overlaps conceptually and cognitively with 'positivism' as a characterisation of social science modelled on the natural sciences. In turn, in so far as many versions of functionalism share a 'positivist' conception of social science (in this sense) then it too shares an area of interlock with empiricism. The same can be argued for the notion of middle-range theory – it shares core areas of commonality and interlock at the conceptual and cognitive levels, and in fact shall give an empirical example of this later in the discussion. Of course, it hardly needs to be said that while these different clusterings or bodies of ideas share these propertiies, they remain distinct and different from each other because their contents are not restricted to such commonalities. As a fundamental theory of knowledge 'empiricism' is germane to many different substantive discourses, including common-sense understanding. Whilst functionalism may possess a naturalist conception of social science, as a theoretical framework it conveys much more than this about the institutional workings of society; and so on.

A crucial distinction to be borne in mind here is that some of these conceptual networks are more exclusively concerned with epistemological matters, whilst others represent both epistemological and ontological elements, but have a greater concentration of ontological elements. Thus, empiricism and rationalism as theories of knowledge, and positivism, humanism and realism as models of social science, contain and deal with mainly epistemological elements such as prescriptions about valid forms of knowledge, theories of truth, the nature of social scientific propositions and so on. Other discourses, for example, theoretical 'schools' such as functionalism, and methodological protocols, whilst they depend upon an infrastructure of such epistemological matters, they also concern themselves with ontological issues. That is, they contain elements which are pertinent to questions about *the nature of social reality* as opposed to questions concerned with how we come to know this reality and what is the

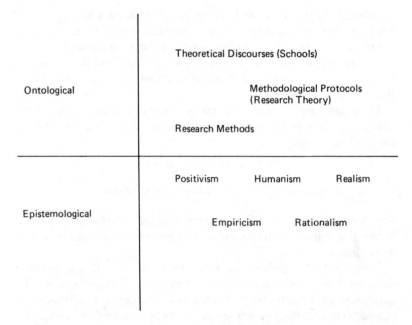

FIGURE 4.1   *Epistemological and Ontological Levels of Discourse*

correct form of this knowledge. Thus, social theoretical discourses contain ideas and concepts about the way in which society is constituted and operates and have a large ontological component. In that methods and methodological protocols enunciate the appropriate analytic units (data) and strategies for collecting data, they thus possess less ontological content than theoretical discourses, but more than purely epistemological ones. Thus, diagrammatically, levels of discourse can be represented as in Figure 4.1

The crux of my unease about Platt's assumptions regarding the general relations between theory and method can be understood precisely in these terms. By concentrating on the validity or otherwise of the *causal* relation between particular theoretical discourses and particular methods, attention is skewed away from other highly important connections which do not show up in this kind of examination. Just as Platt successfully demonstrates the lack of a specifically causal connection between functionalism and the survey, so too, my own model would suggest that at the ontological level there are no *necessary* rational connections between particular social theoretical discourses and particular 'methods' (or even methodological prescriptions). In *that sense and at that level* Platt is right to suggest that what rational connections do exist between theories and methods are ones of 'mere affinity' or 'tendencies to be associated'. However, in the context of the whole model as I have outlined it, it is wrong to make this a *generalised conclusion* about the relation between theory and method.

Thus, although there are no *necessary* rational connections between particular theoretical discourses and methods at an *ontological* level, such as:

functionalism ⟶ survey

or, symbolic interactionism ⟶ participant observation

this does not preclude the necessary rational interlocks that occur between common elements in the epistemological infrastructure of these discourses.

These provide *indirect* or *submerged* aspects of the relation between theoretical discourses and methods as well as between the epistemological components themselves considered as distinct discourses. These cannot be written off as 'mere affinities' or 'tendencies to be associated'; they are, as I have said, *acausal interdependencies* or *necessary* interlocks produced through the mutual sharing of concepts, and thus cognitive and perceptual properties. (This latter notion of linguistic influence on cognition and perception draws upon the linguistic relativity thesis developed by Whorf 1964.) Thus, by focussing upon the explicate order of causal (non-causal) relations between theoretical discourses and methods, the implicate order of acausal interdependencies is masked (see Figure 4.2).

The implicate order at the epistemological level reveals a core of infrastructural interlocks between functionalism and the survey which is ignored if one focusses on the explicate (causal) order. My central point is that such rational connections should be considered *on a par* with causal aspects of the relation between theory and method since they *indirectly* fashion links between theoretical and methodological discourses through acausal interdependencies. The distinction between epistemological and ontological levels of discourse (and thus, between implicate and explicate orders is of paramount importance here and lack of attention to this nuance of my argument can lead to gross misunderstandings and misrepresentations of what I am saying. I am not asserting a simple rational connection between functionalism and the survey as both Platt (1988) and Bulmer (1988)

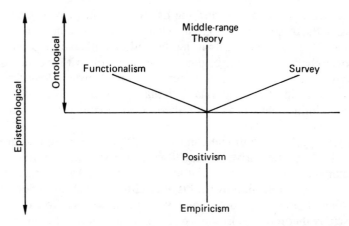

FIGURE 4.2   *Indirect Links between Theory and Method*

suggest. My argument is much more subtle than this, but short of repeating what I have just said, I do not think I can be much clearer (see Appendix).

In the light of these comments we can return to, and evaluate, the substance of Platt's paper. It is very important to bear in mind that when Platt asks the question 'must method imply theory?' (p. 504), or when she suggests that 'the commonplace that method depends on theory is normative, not empirical' (p. 506), that she is defining theory in the restricted way mentioned previously. Also, she is construing the relationship between theory and method in a causal or quasi-causal way which precludes and derogates *necessary* rational connections characterised as acausal relations of interdependence. So, when she says that the general assertion that method implies a theoretical position rests on certain implicit assumptions (p. 504), one has to understand that these generalisations are a product of the above *artificially* imposed constrictions.

In the alternative terms set out above theory and method in general are related in the important senses I have referred to, *without* the attendant implicit assumptions that Platt describes. Thus, in my alternative schema there is no imputation that every theory generates an appropriate method and that 'no additional creativity is required to develop a method, and that methods have no social base or process of social development independent of that for theories' (p. 505). The acausal rational connectedness that I have indicated does not imply a 'perfect fit' between theorising and research methods, but does imply overlaps in, or interlocking of core assumptions at different levels in the discourses. Also, quite clearly methods *do* have independent social bases and they can lag behind or anticipate movements in social theory, but none of these is incompatible with the idea that methods are theory-saturated in terms of their epistemological (and 'social scientific') assumptions and that these indirectly make for 'compatibilities' between certain theoretical discourses and methods at the ontological level.

Whilst proposing rational connections which are more than mere affinities, my alternative account does *not* hold with the view that fundamental theoretical commitments must determine practice in some causal sense. Moreover, this alternative account does not insist or depend upon the idea that 'everyone has a worked out and conscious theoretical position' (p. 506) or that they act consistently and choose methods on theoretical grounds unconstrained by practical considerations. Again, however, to reject all these as necessary assumptions does not mean that there are no implicit theoretical/epistemological assumptions in a persons' position or practice and which connect these assumptions to other positions and assumptions. To suggest otherwise would be to imply that researchers work in an intellectual vacuum devoid of prevailing 'climates of opinion' defined through bodies of ideas. Also, to choose a method for reasons of practicality in no way demonstrates that the method itself is not enmeshed in theoretical/epistemological presuppositions.

It is because Platt's analysis rejects the importance and/or existence of the implicate order of rational connectedness, and the intrinsic link between this and the explicate order of actual empirical *instances* of practice, that her analysis excludes these from the historical investigation of the relations between theory and method. For Platt, 'historical answers are needed to historical questions, epistemological answers to epistemological ones' (private communication). Thus, the historical/empirical contingency account is decisive in relation to historical issues concerning the relation between theory and method because it already precludes (in Platt's definition) epistemological concerns. I want to argue that this severance is entirely arbitrary, since all discourses (whether methodological, epistemological or theoretical) are inextricably subserved as I have attempted to show by lower level epistemological presuppositions.

It is for this reason that I find Platt's use of interview materials with practitioners of particular theories and methods to be insufficient as the basis for comprehensive and generalised statements about the relations between theory and method. Of course, this is entirely consistent from Platt's own point of view, given that she has already precluded the relevance of epistemological questions; but if this assumption is questioned, as I feel it must be, then the *privileged role* which she accords to actors' accounts must also be questioned.

Thus, the use of actors accounts as the only true way of understanding the connections between theory and method because it is grounded in the concrete links between 'adherents' (of theory) and 'users' (of method) must be questioned. Above all, this approach centralises the *actors' story* in the arbitration of the relations between the discourses of theory and method. One is required to abandon speaking of rational connections between these discourses on the grounds that this is either an inherently ideological practice (normative) or simply causally unimportant, and instead, speak of empirical connectedness validated by the actual (historical) actors concerned. That is, in terms of the way Platt 'measures' these links, for example, whether the actors themselves perceived compatibilities between particular theories and methods and whether they mutually read, used and otherwise drew upon them.

Thus, her account does not accord any particular significance to rational connections between theory and method and defers to nothing other than empirically arbitrated ones. If the actors involved *say* there was no connection and indeed if there is no apparent 'fusion' manifest in their published works, then we must conclude that there *are no* important connections between particular theories and methods.

This approach manifestly undervalues many of the rational connections that can be adduced between theory and method both in general and also in the particular case of functionalism and methodological practices other than and including the survey method. Unwittingly, Platt tends to collude with her respondents here because she underestimates the extent to which her respondents have already been affected by their own theoretical and methodological predilections and commitments. She tends to forget that there are ideological, theoretical and epistemological interests and commitments which functionalists and survey researchers share in the first place and which undercut their assumed ideological impartiality. These common interests and commitments can be seen to crystallise around three tightly integrated conceptual 'packages' or clusters.

The first of these is an empiricist conception of knowledge which is associated with a substantivist or eclectic attitude to theorising in a general sense. The empiricist conception of knowledge insists that there is no knowledge independent of sensory experience which is, at the same time, informative about the world. Thus, empiricism denies the validity of other forms of knowledge (such as the implicate order of rational connections) which do not depend upon the truth or falsity of given observational data (Benton 1977, p. 22; Willer and Willer 1973; Layder 1985).

In social scientific terms empiricism accords with the view that theoretical statements must be generated from direct scrutiny of the 'variables', found in the empirical world. In this sense, theory provides a logical organisation of the empirical facts as they are uncovered in specific research projects (Harré and Secord 1972). In this sense, social theory has a fairly narrow province defined in and through the particular substantive areas that it is intended to illuminate. Each substantive area such as suicide, role-behaviour, organisations and so on will produce its own generic theories through the observational testing provided by empirical research. More formal versions of such theory may be obtained by rewriting techniques (Glaser and Strauss 1967) or by using bits and pieces of other 'established' theories in an eclectic or 'decorative' way (a phenomenon which Platt has herself noted, p. 529).

The second package or conceptual cluster associated with both functionalism and the survey is a positivist conception of scientific method as it applies to the social sciences, with the associated ideology of an assumed universality of the applicability of this 'method'. A corollary is the assumption that the social world can be treated in the same 'factual' and 'objective' sense as can the natural world of inanimate objects (Durkheim 1982) and thus there is a virtual disregard for the role of actors 'meanings' in social research (Cicourel 1964; Douglas 1971). Also, given this premise, the desirability of hypothetico-deductive forms of theorising on the basis of empirical observations and generalisations is endorsed.

The third assumptive package that ties in with this network of commitments is an adherence to, and endorsement of, middle-range theory as a methodological protocol. Merton first drew attention to the specifics of systematic theories of the middle-range (1968). It is interesting to note that although Merton was a great champion of functionalist theory, as well as middle-range theory, and although the examples he cites of the latter – such as 'role-set theory' theories of 'social differentiation', and 'institutional interdependence' or 'anomie theory' – have a great affinity with functionalism in general, the two are not necessarily or inevitably tied at the ontological (or object-reference) levels of the discourses. The rational connection between them is produced through the sharing of epistemological assumptions about the nature and forms of sociological knowledge.

Middle-range theory is an example of what I would term 'research-theory' and represents a *level* of theorising which specifies in advance the form and nature of theoretical propositions as they emerge from the research process. As such middle-range theory draws together empiricism and positivism in the form of a methodological protocol. Merton's classical depiction of theories of the middle-range suggests they are developed through hypothetico-deductive forms of theorising on the basis of empirical observations and generalisations, and aim for precision, predictive power and testability, preferably through the use of statistical methods (note here the more than 'mere' affinity with the survey method). Also, the 'middle-range' scope of such theory (between the minor working hypotheses of everyday life and the all-inclusive grand, 'speculative' theories) has the effect of encouraging a substantivist or eclectic approach to the theoretical enterprise in sociology. That is, middle-range theory (for instance, Durkheim's theory of suicide) derives initially from the observation of empirical uniformities or generalisations (for instance, in a number of different populations Catholics have a lower suicide rate than Protestants). Then, by conceptualising this in relation to abstract propositions of a higher order, a predictive, precise and testable theory emerges to account for the observed generalisations. Thus, although there are elements of such theories that can or may be generalised, for instance, a general theory of 'reference groups' or 'role-conflict', the theories themselves are specific to the substantive areas from which they derive and which they subsume.

A good example of a piece of empirical research which ties in all the elements in this conceptual package, that is, empiricism, positivism, functionalism, middle-range theory, substantivism and the survey method is Gross *et al.* (1958) *Explorations in Role Analysis: Studies of the School Superintendency Role.* The middle-range, substantive specificity of the theory of role behaviour and role conflict which the authors develop from research into school superintendents, ensures its compatibility with functionalism at the epistemological level whilst the notion of role itself has affinities and compatibilities with the traditional substantive propositions of functionalism. However, more important than the substantive link with functionalism are the shared epistemological and scientistic premises which exemplify the rational interlocks of the implicate order. The use of the survey method and statistical techniques in the gathering of data from the interviewees articulates well with the positivist conception of social scientific method which undergirds the study. Thus, one of the basic criticisms of this type of study focusses on the inattention to the emergent nature of actors meanings and the problematic nature of everyday behaviour in the attempt to generate scientific statements about behaviour on an objective, external basis through the administration of standardised questionnaire schedules (Cicourel 1964; for further discussion see Appendix).

These shared commitments are displayed by Platt's interviewees and I shall draw attention to some examples of this in a moment. The main point is that instead of recognising these assumptive commitments and then taking them as evidence of the rational connections between various levels of theorising and particular kinds of methodological practice, Platt seems to accept her interviewees accounts at face value as neutral accounts which stress the interviewees' impartiality, and an 'anything goes' attitude to both theory and method. However, if we go beyond the ideological commitments and penetrate below the overt flags of neutrality, we will find that the integrated network of rational connections between empiricism, positivism and middle-range theory serves to preclude other possible forms of knowledge and practice. In serving to expose these lines of cleavage between different discursive associations and assumptive clusters, the seeking out of rational connections performs an important function which is not performed by the method of letting the historical subjects speak for themselves. In fact, this latter method very often obscures these cleavages by creating the façade of a unity of agnosticism.

This highlights the danger of relying solely on actors' accounts in teasing out the manifold relations between theory and method. It also highlights the danger of treating the explicate, causal order as if it was (a) privileged, and (b) completely independent of an implicate order. Thus, Platt's view stresses that unless the actors themselves perceive rational connections, these latter cannot be relevant to their conscious intellectual processes. Such a view does not take into account the fact that the actors concerned may not 'perceive' such connections and their influence on their work for a number of reasons. Ruling out the possibilities of sheer ignorance or even wilful attempts to deny such influences, by far the most important reason for a lack of awareness of such connections would be the *inability* to perceive or cognitively assimilate the implicate order because of 'paradigm blindness' induced by a commitment to a 'world view' based on an explicate causal view of reality. This phenomenon which has been noted by a number of writers (Bohm 1981, p. 46; Feyerbend 1975; Whorf 1964; Kuhn 1962), suggests that the inability to extend awareness beyond the confines of the explicate, manifest order (and thus to see the latter as somehow primary and dominant) results from habituation to the explicate order as it is emphasised in our thought and language; our linguistically mediated 'world view'.

As Bohm points out, an illusion may arise in which the manifest 'content of consciousness is experienced as the very basis of reality and from this illusion one may apparently obtain a proof of the correctness of that mode of thought in which this content is taken to be fundamental' (1981, p. 206–7). Clearly, in the context of such perceptual blind-spots or blockages, there is a very real danger involved in *relying* on actors' accounts for an ideologically uncontaminated description of the 'influences' on their work.

Let us look at examples of empiricism and its attendant substantivism and theoretical eclecticism in Platt's interviewees. In section (iv) of her paper Platt asks 'were survey researchers functionalists?' and suggests on the basis of the evidence that generally they were not. Sometimes they were psychological in orientation and thus not functionalists in the sociological sense, as was the case with Rosenberg's *Occupational Values* (1957). Alternatively, where some functionalist statements do occur in the work of survey researchers functionalism was used 'merely as an available resource which may be drawn on in an eclectic way to illuminate a substantive topic' (p. 521). The work of James, Davis, Glock and Heller can be viewed in this light (p. 520–1). In cases where survey researchers make no reference to functionalist ideas at all their orientation is described as 'theory-free', as in the case of Lundberg whose post-war empirical articles are described by Platt as 'theory-free sociometric accounts of patterns of friendship choice' (p. 517).

Now while such evidence may be used to illustrate the fact that such authors did not necessarily commit themselves to formal statements of functionalist theory (and the very heterogeneity of such formal statements of functionalist orthodoxy makes this improbable anyway), it cannot be adduced that survey researchers did not share with functionalists the underpinning assumptions of empiricist substantivism and theoretical eclecticism. That is, an observed empirical uniformity pertinent to a particular substantive area (suicide, role-sets, friendship choices, and the like) would typically be the research focus, and its investigation (along with the hypothetico-deductive method), would determine theoretical pertinence. This, of course, is the classic statement that Merton makes in relation to middle-range theory (1968). As I have said, theories of the middle-range tend to be defined in terms of researchable substantive areas.

This is the crucial assumptive link between survey research and functionalism; not a putative agreement about the unique appropriateness of survey research for functional theory (see Merton's statement in Platt, p. 513). In fact, it is clear from Platt's own data that no such neat concordance existed. What does exist and is masked by Platt's determined emphasis on the historical contingency of theory/method connections is the idea that the empirical world and empirical phenomena in general set the terms of the theoretical instruments which then proceed to capture the phenomena themselves within an explanatory account. Thus Merton, utilising Durkheim's procedure in his study of suicide, exhorts the would-be middle-range theorist to begin from an observed regularity, say between suicide rate and religious affiliation, and then to generate hypothetico-deductively, a theoretical system which can account for this, for instance degree of social integration of religious groupings and the relation between this and psychic support of group members.

As to the generality of the acceptance of the ideology and conceptual and methodological baggage of the basic assumptions of middle-range theory, there is no doubt. Platt's own data bear this out admirably. Stouffer, who (along with Lazarsfeld) Platt describes as a generally recognised leader of the survey, is described as seeing the desirability of 'middle-range hypotheses' (p. 519). Also, Haller from Wisconsin, a faculty with a strong survey tradition, prompts the following comment from Platt: 'his group saw themselves as testing theories predominantly of a middle-range kind' (p. 521).

The hypothetico-deductive method mentioned in relation to Merton is the final link in the chain of rational connections between different levels of theory and method in the work of functionalists and survey researchers. The hypothetico-deductive method was by no means exclusive to functionalists such as Durkheim and Merton, but that is the point; it is this conception of theoretical production which ties them to others of a positivist-empiricist persuasion including survey researchers and non-sociologists alike (for example, psychologists and social psychologists). The belief in this deductive form of theorising along with an associated 'objectivity' of observational method, provided the backbone of an orthodox hegemonic attitude to social scientific research. Only recently has the positivist account been challenged by a fully-fledged alternative account of naturalism, that is, in the guise of realism. However, I would argue that while not providing an alternative account of naturalism, various humanist strands of social scientific research have historically provided a non-naturalist alternative to the positivist version (Blumer 1956, 1969; Rock 1979) – while retaining a link via an empiricist conception of knowledge (see Layder 1985). Again, the existence of these alternative integrated clusters or conceptual package underlines the importance of the mapping out of rational connections between differing conceptions and levels of theory and method and which indeed remain hidden if we simply approach the problem as one of empirical contingency.

It is only by tracing different clusters of rational connections between epistemological assumptions, different visions of social science, different theoretical discourses, and different methodological protocols and research practices, that one can understand the profound internal disagreements that exist in social science today. In particular, it is only in these terms that one can actually understand Ben-David's statement that there was a post-war 'unifying professional consensus around the ideas of scientific method and morality' (Platt, p. 523), as pointing to a consensus which was relative to a 'perceptual set' governed by the underlying grouping of assumptions that I have already outlined.

As I have already tried to illustrate, the different levels of theorising are organically connected across the traditional divide between theory and 'method'. One important bridge in this case is what I have called 'research theory'. It is interesting that Platt's analysis either precludes or elides this level because on the one hand, she defines theory at the discursive level I have already indicated in which no methodological implications can be assumed. (Hence, although she did not offer them a definition of theory, many of her interviewees say that functionalism implied no specific method). On the other hand, Platt severs the notion of 'methodology' because;

> If the issue were the relation between methodologies and theories, their implications for each other would be tautological for at least part of the range normally covered by 'theory'. (p. 530, footnote 1)

The above statement implies very strongly that 'method' can be understood as separate and independent from both methodology and theory. Thus, in Platt's terms method is defined primarily as 'theory-free' and neutral.

I strongly disagree with this idea for reasons I hope I have already made plain. I believe the distinction between method and method-ology is basically false in the sense that specific methods are always saturated with methodological prescriptions and thus, theoretical assumptions. Even a seemingly 'neutral', crude definition of the survey method as 'the use of standardised interview schedules to collect data on large samples', on closer inspection, proves to be saturated with theoretical assumptions (remembering that theory is defined here in the multi-levelled way that I indicated previously). Thus, the very use of standardised interview schedules defines in advance both the kind of data it draws attention to, and the kind that it precludes. That is, in terms of the method itself, qualitative data is, by definition (theoretical presupposition) ignored, and quan-titative data is considered primary. This 'foreclosure' thus commits survey research to a positivist, as opposed to a humanist, conception of social science with all its attendant presuppositions about the nature of social reality and the form of 'valid' sociological knowledge (see, for instance, the phenomenological critique of positivist methods in Cicourel 1964, Douglas 1971).

Apart from these 'internal' presuppositions, it is also important to realise that to define methods in the abstract is to falsely separate them from research practice(s) in the more general (and pragmatic) sense. Thus, particular methods are never used outside the context of the investigation of particular substantive areas. This fact forges possible links with either or both of two types of theoretical presup-positions. The first derives from the fact that the method which 'taps into' a particular substantive area does so in a way which is 'directed' by extant theory or theoretical ideas germane to the particular sub-stantive area. Thus, an empirical study of suicide will be directed to *certain kinds* of data on the basis of established (tested) theoretical and empirical knowledge of the area.

Alternatively, in the absence of a body of established knowledge or theory relating to the substantive area in question, the research method or strategy will be guided or directed by one of two possibilit-ies. Either it will be guided by an ethic of substantivism, that is, that the theory will be generated from the substantive area in question, or it will be guided by a more general theoretical system, for example, functionalism, Marxism, and the like. Whatever is the case, such sensitising antennae are necessary to produce the explanatory content of research reports and the documentation of 'findings'. Without them, methods in the abstract could take nothing but a blind stab at the potentially infinite complexity of social reality and, moreover, produce nothing but a meaningless jumble of literally 'raw' data.

A full characterisation of the relation between theory and method must recognise the theoretical/rational bridges between the traditional division of theory and method, and it is this that the notion of 'research theory' tries to do. As I have said, research theory defines the form in which theory must appear as the outcome of the research process. The ideology of middle-range theory (and I am not suggesting that it is merely an ideology) is a very clear example of this. It is crucial to note that Merton, the main champion of middle-range theory, is also a leading functionalist. While it is essential to remember that one does not have to be a functionalist to use middle-range theory or vice versa, there is a strong compatibility between both middle-range theory and functionalism, and middle-range theory and survey research.

Another example of research theory is 'grounded theory' which was, at least in part, developed as an alternative to many of the limitations imposed by middle-range theory (see Glaser and Strauss 1967). In the case of grounded theory however, while there is an empiricist basis to its epistemological infrastructure (although the empiricism takes a slightly different form to that of functionalism), the humanist vision of social science on which it is based is entirely different from the positivist version upon which middle-range theory, functionalism and survey research are based (see Layder 1982). While being a grounded theorist *ipso facto* does not preclude the use of survey methods (as functionalism does not finally preclude participant observation), there are philosophical and practical compatibilities between grounded theory and participant observation which ensure their more than historically contingent connection.

The fundamental point is that both middle-range theory and grounded theory are enmeshed in methodological prescriptions and this in itself highlights the need for a multi-levelled conception of theory when speaking of its relation to method. If the prescriptive assumptions of research theory as I call it are not admitted to the definition of theory, then a narrower definition will overlook both the prescriptive (theoretical) assumptions themselves and, more importantly, their implications for research practice.

My main intention above has been to rectify the misassumption

that what I have described as the implicate order of rational interlocks and their relation to practice is somehow less important than,
or subordinate to, the explicate order of casual relations in the
general characterisation of the relations between theory and method.
This misassumption seems to flow from the idea that because the
implicate order is uninformative about causation therefore it is
uniformative (or insignificant) *per se vis-à-vis* integral matters concerning the relation between theory and method. Such a conflation
denies the significance of acausal associative phenomena in general
and the interdependencies between these and the explicate order.

It may be appropriate as a matter of analytic convenience or
strategy to focus attention on the explicate order of casual relations
as *one non-privileged dimension* of the relation between theory and
method, and, as I have said, in this respect I have no quarrel with
Jennifer Platt's construal of the causal aspects of the relation between
functionalism and the survey. However, my basic disagreement
emerges when the effects and significance of the implicate order are
ignored or denigrated, or arbitrarily severed from a general account
of the relations between theory and method.

MISUNDERSTANDING CAUSALITY IN REALISM

So far the discussion has centred on two main notions; that of a
distinct but complementary relation between causal and acausal
phenomena and between implicate and explicate orders of reality. I
want now to return to the discussion at the beginning of this chapter
and attempt to draw out some further implications. But first let me
recapitulate. In the preliminary section of this chapter I began by
endorsing the realist model of causation as a superior account to the
positivist notion of constant conjunctions of events. Thus, the realist
search for generative (causal) mechanisms which have intrinsic
powers to produce specific effects when activated or stimulated is a
search for genuinely explanatory mechanisms rather than descriptions of (nonetheless existent) regularities in successions of pairs of
events.

I quoted the example given by Wilson (1982) of the breaking of
a glass by a flying rock, and the fact that a concern with causal
mechanisms should concentrate on the molecular structure of the
glass as the important causal mechanism whilst the flying rock should
be seen as the external stimulus for the activation of this mechanism.

Thus, the question 'why does the glass break?' must be answered in terms of both the causal mechanism (the molecular structure of the glass) *and* the stimulation event (the flying rock). In this model causal mechanisms possess powers in the *latent* sense that while they always possess these powers, they are only activated under specific circumstances.

Now while I think that this example does convey the advantages of the realist model of causality, once we substitute an example from the social world rather than the natural world, the model can be subject to misunderstandings and misinterpretations. This is partly related to the problem I broached in relation to the use of examples from physical science on the question of the viability of the notion of 'practical adequacy' as an alternative to the notion of truth or cognitive adequacy. The social world is very different from the physical world as authors from Weber onwards have emphasised and thus, what applies to one in the form of a particular example, may not apply to the other. Again, this involves the vexed question of ontology, and in this specific case it relates to the difference in the nature of social as against natural or physical reality.

Thus, in the hands of someone unfamiliar with the subtleties of the problems of the transposition of such examples, the 'flying rock' case may be completely misinterpreted as applying to social reality in the form of an argument about 'blaming the victim'. For example, take the case of rape. If one literally transposes the flying rock example, one could come up with the ludicrous assertion that the rape victim (the analogue to the glass jar) is the cause (causal mechanism) of the rape itself and not the attacker (the analogue to the external stimulation event which activates the causal mechanism).

I suggest above that this is a ludicrous assertion, but it is just the sort of suggestion that has been put forward in many official judicial pronouncements on such issues; that it is the woman's fault, she was 'asking for it'. Now I want to make it clear that the realist notion of causality is not and cannot be an endorsement of the 'blaming the victim' assertion and really has nothing to do with a realist notion of causality as I interpret it. Such a confusion would arise from a number of misassumptions. For example, this would be the case when it is assumed (wrongly) that there is an identity between the ontological structures of the social and natural worlds such that the things that 'happen' to people are inevitably the result of internal causal mechanisms. It hardly needs to be pointed out that although people have some responsibility for their own behaviour, the situation of the rape victim and her attacker is a social one involving human beings with varying objectives and intentions. It is quite unlike the natural world of inanimate objects which act upon each other independently of such things as the consciousness and motivations of the objects concerned, not the least because the objects concerned do not possess such properties.

These qualities are exclusive to the world of human interaction and as such as may become causal loci in themselves. Thus, in most cases, rape is quite clearly the result of the aggressive intent of a rape-motivated male and has nothing to do with a self-induced event resulting from the (conscious or unconscious) desires of the victim. Also, clearly in other cases a person's behaviour towards themselves in specific situations may be said to be causally influential in what happens to them. Thus, certain forms of reactive depression or neurotic behaviour derive from the 'imprisoning' and deluding kind of self-talk that certain individuals engage in (Rowe 1978 and 1983; Lemert 1962). In these cases it is not the individual in a vacuum who is 'causing' themselves to behave in certain ways, but it is the way these individuals are responding to the specific social circumstances in which they find themselves (domestic, friendship, marital, sexual and so on).

The variability of these examples highlights the most important point of all in relation to the question of causality as it applies to the social sphere. That is, *what* is regarded as a causal mechanism in the social world will depend on a whole host of circumstances, none of which are as clear-cut or sharply defined as they are in the natural world. Not the least of the complications involved here centres on the *specifics* as well as the *type* of example that is used to 'display' the causal effects in question. All examples which involve the social behaviour of individuals (or several caught up in situated activity) of course, will require a preliminary investigation into the social meanings and definitions of the activity, and the motivations of those involved, before any causal imputations can be made.

The above discussion has served to pre-empt the possible assertion that a realist account of causality licenses a 'blaming the victim' approach to understanding some aspects of social life. I hope I have demonstrated that such a misinterpretation would be based upon several serious misunderstandings and confusions. However, before the form of my defence is misunderstood in the guise of another possible objection, let me quickly reiterate what I have said already at several points. Current realist writing has concentrated too much on the causal powers of human beings and this has led various writers to overestimate the degree to which people are engaged in constructing the world in which they live. In turn, this has given rise to two dominant strands within realist writing. The first strand views human agents as the exclusive loci of causality (evident in the work of Harré and his followers), while the second strand has tried to incorporate structural or institutional aspects, but has done so in a rather ambiguous way. In the next chapter I am critical of both these approaches, although I have much more sympathy with the latter position.

CAUSAL MECHANISMS OR GENERATIVE NETWORKS?

The objective for a general realist position which meets both the cognitive and practical needs of macro and micro analyses in social science is not only a widening of the domain of causal concerns (and this relates to the argument in the next chapter concerning the need for an extended conception of social ontology) but also, as I have argued earlier, a widening of focus to incorporate acausal phenomena. Earlier in this chapter I distinguished between acausal phenomena which can be regarded as generative loci and non-causal phenomena which are not and thus have no particular explanatory status.

As I said, although acausal phenomena are generative in that they have powers and produce effects, these have to be understood in a quite different way from the causal model proposed in realist writing and which is represented in figure 4. 3.

In my discussion of the implicate order I have tried to describe a form of generative influence which breaks from this linear-chain

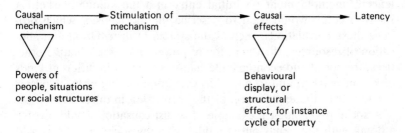

FIGURE 4.3 *Causation in Realism*

notion of causality; thus I used the term acausality in relation to the implicate order. This acausality operates through the activation of the powers of particular phenomena (such as the rational interlocking of epistemological elements and the relation between these and the practice of individual researchers). Thus, there is a diffuse and mutual interchange of influences produced through the interaction of different kinds of phenomena. I went on to suggest that the relationship between the explicate order of causality and the implicate order of acausality has to be expressed in an acausal way. In this manner I have attempted to stretch the boundaries of what are taken to be generative phenomena of most concern to realism, not by abandoning or disregarding the realist concern with causality, but by suggesting the existence of an order of phenomena in tandem with and thus complementary to causal concerns.

But what of the causal domain itself; the explicate order? Does the notion of acausality as I have described it have any implications for a realist causal account? I think it does but again, I am not arguing for a complete abandonment of the existing model; rather, I am proposing an adjunct to it. The great advance that realist accounts of causality have over positivist regularity accounts is that they endeavour to go beyond the registration of correlated events as if they represented the causal mechanism itself. Thus, in a realist account the description of constant conjunctions of pairs of events (that is, basically a statement of correlation) is supplanted by an attempt to specify *why* such correlations exist by reference to the generative mechanisms which produce them.

To take a sociological example, a realist account of social inequalities would want to go beyond the establishment of correlations between indices related to inequality such as that between low socio-economic status of parents, the low educational attainment of their children and the likelihood of these offspring subsequently experiencing unemployment on initial entry into the labour market. A realist account would want to describe the mechanisms which produce these correlations, such as the system of distribution and allocation of resources, the operation of power and discriminative practices, the social and economic mechanisms at work in different kinds of labour market, and so on, whichever combination of mechanisms is relevant to the explanation of the correlation in question.

A social psychological example of realist causation would involve a break with the behaviourist model whereby social activity is said to be triggered by an environmental stimulus which leads to a conditioned response by the individual. It would also involve a break with much experimentally-based psychology wherein correlations between experimentally controlled behavioural variables (say between eye gaze, sex, and social status, and so on) which, although in many cases are based on careful experimentation, often tend to be treated in a manner which suggests that they express causal relationships.

In other words, they tend to imply more about causation than is warranted by the accumulated evidence of correlations between variables. A realist social psychology would wish to focus on the intentionality, self-monitoring procedures and general skilfulness of human beings as transformers of environmental inputs (Harré and Secord 1972). Associated with these features is the human's ability to choose courses of action in terms of the possibilities that they envisage to be appropriate (for example, having strategic advantage in the situation, or being in accordance with deeply-held beliefs), rather than dictated to by some pre-programmed script.

Without doubt the realist account of causation attempts to go beyond the descriptive level implicit in the search for 'constant conjunctions of pairs of events' or the correlations between personality or social structural variables' by employing the metaphor of generative mechanisms with intrinsic powers which may or may not be activated. However, there is an even more basic metaphor which forges a link between positivist and realist versions of causality. This is the metaphor of a punctuated linear-chain produced through the follow-on effects of one phenomenon on another. The positivist conception of causality utilises this metaphor in the form of successions of pairs of events, but the realist conception reproduces it in the form of the activation of the powers of generative mechanisms and their ability to produce new phenomena or transform existing phenomena.

The punctuated linear-chain metaphor which is reproduced in the realist model (see figure 4:3) does not necessarily rule out the notion of causal feedback loops such that the effects set in motion by specific generative mechanisms stimulate the powers of other mechanisms which, in turn, act back on the original mechanism. (It must be said that the same is true for the notion of successions of pairs of events.) However, both the feedback version and the unidirectional version of causality implicit in the realist model, can be characterised as punctuated linear-chains of *effects*. That is, the relevant phenomena and the connections between them (such as generative mechanisms, sources of activation and the resultant created or transformed phenomena) are separated in time and space.

With the model of generative networks that I want to propose, the basic requirement would be to break with the linear-chain meta-phor and adopt a more mosaic conception of 'generative influences'. One of the most powerful resistances to such an idea derives from the fact that the linear-chain metaphor is so deeply embedded in our language, thought and speech. Whorf (1964) emphasised the linear view of time that is engendered by the structure of European langu-ages like English and which is reflected in the cultural importance of clocks, calendars and diaries.

In relation to the discussion of the implicate order I have already drawn attention to Bohm's idea that our linguistic habits and the world view mediated by our language are pivotal in his distinction between an implicate and explicate order as applied to physical reality. I suggest that this is just as true for the social world. The notion of an explicate or manifest order of causality as a linear succession of events or effects is built into our social scientific, linguis-tic habits. Another aspect of Bohm's point is that resistances to the abandonment of the linear-chain view may be the result of a per-ceptual or cognitive blinkeredness produced through the constraining force of linguistic habits. That is, the use of certain forms of language allows us to 'see' or understand the importance of some things at the same time as obscuring or masking the existence and/or import-ance of others. Thus, to repeat what Bohm says, an illusion may arise in which the manifest 'content of consciousness is experienced as the very basis of reality' (1981, p206–7).

It is in relation to such (linguistically mediated) habitual ways of thinking about the social world and social causation in particular that the idea of a mosaic or network of generative loci, I anticipate, will be met with a fair amount of resistance. Notwithstanding this I wish to propose such a model with respect to the explicate order of social reality. I must stress here that I am using the term 'explicate' in a slightly different way to Bohm. By this term I wish to refer to the ontological items of the social world. That is, I use the term 'explicate order' to refer to the real phenomena that exist in the social world and bear some relation to the status and doing of human social activity.

However, I must immediately enter the caveat that this is not to say that the ontological features of the social world are restricted to the domain of human doing or being. The crucial qualification here is contained in the phrase *'bear some relation* – to being and doing'. In my opinion other, relatively impersonal and relatively independent phenomena such as social structures, or situational or organisational contexts, or Third-World cultural phenomena must be included within the embrace of the phrase 'the ontological features of the social world'. (See the next chapter for a more detailed account.)

The inclusiveness of this definition carries with it the implication that ontological features may be both 'manifest' in the sense of being immediately apparent to our sensory apprehension (such as various forms of being and doing) as well as underlying, or relatively unobservable features, such as social structures or various forms of social organisation such as labour markets, which elude the practical or everyday perception of those people working within them, or at least who are subject to their influence in some way. In this manner the explicate order relates to ontological features which may be underlying (partly hidden), like the generative mechanisms of realism, but also manifest, like various forms of social behaviour or styles of interaction, and which may in some cases be understood (at least in part) as the causal effects of such phenomena.

Thus, at the same time as utilising Bohm's distinction between implicate and explicate orders, I want to cut across it by insisting that for my purposes (that is, as applied to social reality), the distinction should not be predicated solely on the idea of a manifest/hidden dichotomy. However, in saying this I do not want to be understood as adopting the opposite extreme, asserting that the dichotomy is of no importance at all in depicting the distinction between the implicate and explicate orders. This may appear to be confused and contradictory, but it is not. Perhaps the matter can be cleared up by saying that I take the defining features of the implicate and explicate orders as they relate to the social world to be embedded in the distinction between epistemological and ontological features and levels of analysis.

Defined in this way the distinction is totally consonant with the discussion throughout this chapter. The issue of the relation between theory and method which constituted the bulk of the earlier sections concentrated on rational interlocks at an *epistemological level* and which underlay and subserved the depiction, construal and application of research methods and practices. Thus, the implicate order refers to an epistemological infrastructure which cognitively underpins an ontological order of manifest theories, methods, protocols and research strategies. In this sense the implicate (epistemological) order is hidden and underlying and is not necessarily manifest in the day-to-day consciousness of practitioners.

However, if we take the explicate order to refer to the ontological features of the social world as I have defined them, then while in general these are more sensorily accessible as compared with epistemological phenomena, nonetheless, particular ontological features may be more or less manifest or underlying as the case may be. This seeming diversion is important for my argument about the compatibility between the realist version of causation and the network model of generative loci that I am proposing (see Figure 4:4).

In relation to this model I do not want to jettison the important realist idea that causal mechanisms *may* be, to greater and lesser degrees underlying and generative. However, I do want to break from the idea that the effects of causal powers are always or necessarily produced through linear-chain sequences. Thus, in the network

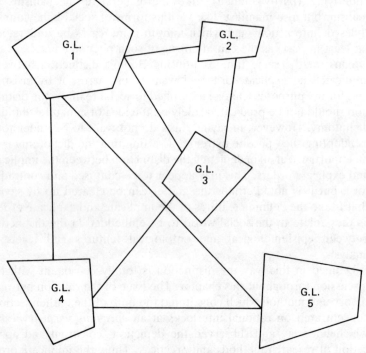

Boxes contain different generative units/mechanisms/phenomena.
Lines represent degree of connectedness and interdependence

FIGURE 4.4   *A Network of Generative Loci*

model the descriptive epithets of 'punctuation' and 'linearity' as applied to the linked units involved in the causal sequence are replaced by others such as 'diffuseness' and 'mutuality' of generative influences, which more appositely express the interchanges between phenomena which are linked to each other in terms of varying degrees of strength and dependency.

Thus, the time-space separations that are an integral feature of the linear-chain model are abandoned in favour of a model in which the component units meld into one another in respect of their generative effects. It is difficult to find a descriptive language which can reflect this somewhat alien way of thinking, but something like the 'simultaneous mutuality of influences' is suggestive of the unbroken continuity of connections between generative phenomena.

This is not to say that at some point in the analysis of a specific empirical problem, for example the 'determinants of young adults labour market status' (see later example) one cannot assign priority or dominance to one influence (or factor) or set of influences rather than others. This will be a matter that can only be decided at some point later in the analysis of data. What it does mean is that one cannot assume prior to the investigation of a particular causal sequence which aspect of the network one would want to designate as more or less important in relation to the whole configuration.

However, even at a later stage of analysis where some priorities have been assigned to particular units or sectors of the configuration, I must stress that we are dealing only with relative strengths of association and direction of influence, we are not talking about clearly delineated punctuations or separations in the overall network. I shall now present an example of the kind of empirical research problem that reflects these features.

In this case the constituent empirical and theoretical units in the network (generative loci and interdependencies) are known or defined in advance of the research project (although specific details of the data-sets have to be carefully sampled and controlled), but the exact generative relations between the units of the network are not known. In other words the researcher devises a research project that will enable him or her to make statements about the relative strengths of influence of specific generative mechanisms within the network under specific circumstances. Only in this way will a general account of the powers of the generative units in relation to the others in the network emerge from the interplay of theory and research.

With respect to the specific problem of the investigation of the operation of labour markets, the powers and likely effects of specific units or loci will be known in advance. The following would be examples of this: the proposition that segmented labour markets provide strong barriers to mobility (Krekel 1980; Layder 1984), or the proposition that some types of industrial organisation ensure minimum worker conformity to organisational rules by providing incentives (pay and status gradings) for 'good' behaviour (Edwards 1979). However, many of these generative loci will be formed under varying circumstances, that is, in networks with various combinations of types of loci in many specific forms.

Take the example mentioned earlier, the determinants of young adults' labour market status. This will involve investigating the relationship between 'individual attributes' such as 'sex', 'age', 'class', 'educational attainment' and so on, and their interaction with structural features such as local and national labour markets, the specific form of their segmentation, their buoyancy or depression, and so forth. Furthermore, the research would involve the analysis of all these factors on the early labour market experiences (work and non-work) of young adults (Ashton *et al.* 1989).

In this example the generative loci are already known in two senses. First, they are empirically identifiable and accessible; thus they can be sampled and, assuming the correct application of certain methodological procedures, data can be produced, in principle, fairly easily (that is, also assuming there are no practical problems or difficulties of access, and so on). This does not imply, however, that the analysis of the data will not pose particular problems and require the use of novel or relatively new statistical or computational techniques.

Second, some of the powers of some of the generative loci or mechanisms are known or can be derived from extant theories of the labour market and power and from the way in which class factors such as family and educational background predispose or channel young people in certain directions through the acquisition of various skills and values. However, what is not known is how all these generative loci interact with each other and subsequently influence the early experiences and labour market status of young adults. Thus, the relative strengths of the connections between loci and the reasons why they exist in the form they do, will emerge during the research process. This will result both from the emergent data itself and from the theoretical explanations generated through the confrontation between the known powers of the generative loci (in specific circumstances) and the reapplication and respecification of these theoretical models in the current research situation.

To trace the generative effects of loci in a network such as this would produce a general model of the whole process one is attempting to investigate and which would be quite unlike a linear-chain sequence. As I have said, the realist notion of causality has broken away from the positivist version of a specific linear-chain (or succession) of events, and has pointed to the very important notion of underlying causal mechanisms possessing powers to produce certain effects when stimulated. However, in my opinion realism has not sufficiently distanced itself from the linear-chain metaphor, and thus this metaphor still underpins its notion of causality in the form;

Causal $\longrightarrow$ Latency $\longrightarrow$ Stimulation $\longrightarrow$ Causal $\longrightarrow$ Latency
Mechanism   Effects

As I hope the above example has demonstrated, the linear-chain metaphor is not flexible enough to allow social scientists to talk about the complex interrelations between generative mechanisms within whole networks of such mechanisms. Thus, I have spoken of 'generative loci' in preference to 'mechanisms' in this respect to emphasise their location within an encompassing network. Understanding generative phenomena in terms of circuits of generative loci (units or mechanisms) and the conduits which bind them together through reciprocal effects and interdependencies, moves away from the one-dimensionality of the linear-chain metaphor. The idea of concatenations of 'causal' loci draws attention to the patterned relations between generative phenomena with causal powers.

Thus, the way forward is not simply to abandon the notion of causality as realism has proposed it, but to understand it as one narrowly focussed aspect of the more general problem of the generative powers and cumulative effects of whole networks of generative phenomena. However, since the very notion of causality is deeply embedded in the linear-chain metaphor, it may be better to think of this mosaic conception as 'networks of generative phenomena' rather than a subspecies of causality. I am being ambivalent here, and deliberately so since I do not want to deny the importance of 'causal mechanisms' as realists have described them. That is, I fully endorse the break that realists have made with the positivist notion of conjunctions of pairs of events, while retaining a general concern with questions of why things are as they are (causality and causal laws) which are associated with a realist conception of social science.

My objective has been to attempt to free the set of concerns which are normally dealt with as aspects of causality from an implicit (and somewhat rigid) adherence to the linear-chain metaphor. The ambivalence in my argument arises as a result of wanting to abandon this metaphor and adopt a mosaic (or network) conception of generative loci. It then becomes a moot question as to whether we should retain the term 'causality' itself while retaining a focus on the phenomena that normally fall within its domain. Therefore, I wish simply to pose it as a question for the future development of realism. If my argument that the realist conception of causality is embedded in a linear-chain metaphor is acceptable, and that therefore a network conception of generative loci is more appropriate or adequate to the typical research problems facing social science, then should we still be using the term causality?

The whole point of a network conception is that the concatenations of generative loci produce emergent generative powers that cannot be understood as an isolated linear sequence of causal effects; they have to be understood as complex interrelations with diffuse reciprocal influences. Also, the relative strengths of influence of specific generative loci have to be understood in terms of the operation of the composite relations of the network and not simply in terms of intrinsic powers which can be defined outside the context of specific networks.

5 Behaviour and Social Ontology

INTRODUCTION

In this chapter I want to turn to some issues connected with the explanation of social behaviour which are crucial to the realist programme. However, by way of introduction to these issues I want to look at the work of Winch and Louch because, I would argue, in a sense they set the agenda for subsequent work on this area, including that of the realists. As a correlate of this I want to argue that the Winch-Louch legacy has left a clear imprint on much realism, sometimes despite protestations to be contrary. The pervasive influence of Winch in particular will be seen also in the discussion in chapter 6 on the relationship between the technical language of social science and common sense.

I then move onto a discussion of the specifically realist approaches to the general question of explanation of social behaviour. In particular I will concentrate on the question of the causal status of actors' reasons and accounts. Whilst realist writing displays some ambiguity and no little variability on this question, all realists, nonetheless, have attempted some explanatory resolution of the problem. This discussion then becomes the platform from which I can deal with questions about social ontology.

I argue that the way realists have attempted to resolve the question of the causal status of actors' reasons/accounts has led them to certain ideas, deficient in my opinion, about the nature of social ontology. The concept that effects the transition between the discussion of actors' accounts and general models of ontology is that of 'social relation'. I suggest that it is worthwhile distinguishing between two major modalities of social relations, each of which is subject to different epistemological connotations. I then defend a neo-objectivist version ('neo', because I distinguish it from so-called naive objectivism' which has affinities with positivism, empiricism and a correspondence theory of knowledge) of the concept against the empiricist versions favoured by many, if not all, realists.

My discontent with current realist general models of social ontology follows from this and thus I use the rest of the chapter to elucidate what I call an 'extended stratified' model. I feel that this model improves upon the extant realist ones in the sense that it opens up the domains of explanatory possibility. In other words, I feel that the realist models on offer have the effect of constricting the explanatory scope and basis of realism in a way which is inessential to the defence of realism as a distinct alternative philosophy of social science.

WINCH'S RATIONALISM AND LOUCH'S MORAL EXPLANATION

In one sense Winch's argument in *The Idea of a Social Science* can be construed as rationalist in that he endorses *a priori* forms of reasoning in social analysis. In so far as I, too, have been pressing the case for a form of rationalism to be adopted by realism it is a matter of interest to trace through exactly what Winch's approach entails. Similarly, in so far as Winch was proposing a radical critique of, and alternative to, the natural science model as applied to the social sciences (namely, positivism) then it is also interesting to see in what respects (if any) there are convergencies between Winch's mode of analysis and that of realism.

In a certain light Winch's argument in *The idea of a Social Science* can be viewed as a species of philosophical counter-imperialism which aims to win back the investigation of social reality for the philosopher, rather than let it remain prey to the methodological crudities of empirical social scientists. In the main, this is because Winch wishes to dislodge what he calls the 'underlabourer' conception of philosophy, whereby philosophy is seen merely as the means of clearing away linguistic confusions and 'preparing the ground' for the more important procedures of empirical (scientific) research. In fact, for Winch philosophy must play the *central* role since philosophy and social study are actually one and the same thing!

In this respect Winch is quite opposed to the application of the methods of natural science to social studies, as is exemplified in Durkheim's studies such as *The Rules of Sociological Method* and *Suicide*. According to Winch, the natural sciences are empirically based and attempt to trace causal relations in human behaviour which are founded upon observed regularities in such behaviour. Such an approach does violence to the *meaningful* nature of social behaviour; that is, the way in which human action can be understood as rule-following behaviour.

It follows from this that instead of being empirical, social study is and must be conceptual in nature, and concern itself with elucidating the meaning of the rules informing human conduct. The method used in social study (as opposed to social *science*) must be that of *verstehen*, whereby the investigator attempts to trace the connections between a person's actions and the meanings expressed in and by those actions. This, claims Winch, is precisely the function of the philosopher: the elucidation of frames of meaning in forms of social life by '*a priori* conceptual analysis rather than by empirical research' (1963, p. 17).

It can be appreciated that Winch's position is meant to be a powerful indictment of the kind of objectivist social study advocated by Durkheim in his methodological and empirical work. Durkheim was led by his naturalism to view social reality as if it were of a dual nature, consisting of both the everyday commonsense worlds of human beings and the 'more profound causes which are unperceived by consciousness' (quoted in Winch 1963, p. 23). These more profound courses, of course, were the 'social facts' which Durkheim felt could not be explained in terms of individuals but rather in terms of 'the manner according to which associated individuals are grouped' (p. 24).

Winch's position is diametrically opposed to this view since he believes that social reality and social relations are entirely conceptual in nature. There are no other 'more profound' or 'external social facts' which exist outside of the expression of ideas about reality; 'A man's social relations with his fellows are permeated with his ideas about reality. Indeed, "permeated" is hardly a strong enough word; social relations are expressions of ideas about reality!' (p. 23). Thus, the objectivist, positivist search for causal laws beyond the consciousness of individuals involved in social life comes into conflict with philosophy 'conceived as an enquiry into the nature of man's knowledge of reality' (p. 24). Since for Winch philosophy is identical with the real aims and 'methods' of social inquiry, positivist social science also conflicts with this 'reconstructed' notion of social inquiry.

In line with the ontological claim that reality is entirely conceptual in nature Winch also insists that social reality and social behaviour must be analysed and understood in terms of concepts which bear some direct relationship to those of the participants under study. I shall deal with this claim in detail in chapter 6 where I discuss the nature of social scientific or 'technical' reasoning as compared with mundane or commonsense reasoning. However, this claim about the intrinsic closeness of observers' and participants' accounts is the argumentative prop on which Winch rescues the analysis of actors' reasons from the dissipations of positivism. Thus, for Winch one of the most insidious features of positivism is its discounting of individuals' reasons, attitudes, concepts and so on, in the explanation of social behaviour.

Within the empirical and research-oriented traditions in social science there have been several parallel attempts to incorporate and establish the importance of actors' perspectives into social analysis and social theory. The most notable of these has been the symbolic interactionist tradition, particularly its Chicago school variant, and various forms of phenomenological or existential sociologies, the most prominent of which has been ethnomethodology whose theoretical programme was instigated by Garfinkel (1967). In many respects these schools have mirrored Winch's concern to elevate the explanatory status of actors' accounts, and to promote a critique of the natural science model; that is, positivism and naive objectivism in the social sciences. However, most crucially, these schools of thought part company with the Winchian thesis over the issue of the role of empirical research. Whereas Winch conceives social analysis as the *a priori* elucidation of frames of meaning, both ethnomethodology and in particular symbolic interactionism have conceived the task of meaning-frame elucidation as irretrievably empirical. That is, they conceive of such elucidation as the informed outcome of direct engagement with the empirical reality of forms of life.

It is because of the radical counter to the received model of social science that is contained within these interpretive sociologies that modern realists and those who associate themselves (or have been associated) with realism have found it necessary to attempt to incorporate an 'interpretive moment' into social analysis. However, I would argue that it is as a direct result of this that in many instances realists have (perhaps unwittingly) embraced an interpretive problematic as the epistemological basis of their reconstituted naturalism, and which has been at the cost of a structuralist or neo-objectivist component. Later in this chapter I argue strongly that such a component *must* play a part in realism at both epistemological and ontological levels. Again, my intention is not to try to abolish or suppress the undeniable interpretive moment of social reality, but to establish a judicious balance between the interpretive and objectivist moments in social analysis in general.

However, for the moment, let us return to Winch's argument. As a corrective to the mechanistic and scientistic assumptions of positivism Winch's position is creditable and as I have said, in this respect has direct affinities with various humanistic strands in sociology and social psychology. However, taken to its extreme, as Winch indeed has, there are a number of drawbacks associated with this form of philosophical humanism. The most serious of these turns on the philosophical imperialism of Winch. It is not simply that Winch envisages and demands a major role for philosophy in the investigation of social reality. In this he is undeniably correct. What is unacceptable, however, is that Winch assumes that philosophical analysis (as he construes it), and social investigation are synonymous; that social investigation has no separate existence outside these specific philosophical terms. Thus, the empirical research component of social analysis is neatly precluded; it becomes a purely philosophical matter of conceptual analysis. Of course, this will not do for those observers of social reality like myself who wish to savour its substantive content, its inner texture so to speak.

A related problem is Winch's extremely myopic conception of philosophical analysis, and here he provides an interesting mixture of discursive influences. Winch identifies himself as being concerned with *a priori* conceptual analysis and, coupled with his rejection of an empirical dimension to social investigation, this suggests that he is a rationalist (of the extreme variety) although he nowhere explicitly states his position in relation to the debate between empiricism and rationalism. If this is an accurate depiction of Winch's position, then there would seem to be a number of possible connections with the position that I have been enunciating throughout this book.

However, closer scrutiny does not bear this out. The only possible area of agreement between myself and Winch concerns the fact that I believe that there are problems associated with the investigation of social reality, which cannot be settled simply by empirical investigation. Even here, the qualification, 'simply' distinguishes my approach from Winch's, which insists on a clean severance between conceptual analysis and the 'contamination' of the empirical world. In so far as I have argued that the dominance of empiricism has had a constricting effect on knowledge in social science, there would seem to be an affinity between my own and Winch's position. However, there is, in fact, little agreement here since I argue that the dominating influence of empiricism should be balanced by a complementary concern with rationalist forms and modes of acquisition of knowledge, whereas Winch argues for a position which supports the complete self-sufficiency of *a priori* forms of reasoning. Clearly, Winch proposes a variant of extreme rationalism which I identified in chapter 3 and which I am keen to avoid.

This kind of extreme rationalism has the effect of asserting or assuming its self-validity by proposing that the objects of its discourse are, quite simply, constructed within the discourse itself. In this case the very general notion of 'conceptual analysis' (which Winch equates with 'philosophical analysis' and/or 'social analysis') is assumed to be the discourse in question and provides the source of all the object-references of the discourse. As can be appreciated, such a position may endorse many forms of ill-disciplined assertions about the nature of empirical forms of life, as long as they can be identified as in conformity with 'conceptual analysis', since there is no requirement that such an analysis must be informed by external, empirical, object-referents.

Louch (1966) has proposed a variant of this thesis which endeavours to side-step the extreme *a priori* and anti-empirical stand of Winch's position. Louch contends that it is necessary to explain human behaviour as a form of moral explanation. True explanation of human action does not reside in the (positivist) attempt to formulate generalisations based on atomistic sense data. Rather, it depends upon; '*ad hoc* pronouncements which we make with confidence about the motives and intentions, desires and anxieties, the anticipated pleasures and felt pains which account for this or that human action' (p. 38).

According to Louch when we offer explanations for human behaviour 'we are seeing the behaviour as justified by the circumstances in which it occurs' (p. 4); thus, what counts as 'evidence' or a 'datum' is governed by the context of the behaviour concerned. It is this 'contextual' nature of action which lends itself to observational analysis and thus away from the extreme *a priorism* of Winch's position. Louch agrees that moral explanation is not something that would 'benefit from the strategies which one would enlist in order to establish the probability, of a causal hypothesis' (p. 175) – that is statistical sampling and the search for causal probabilities. However, this should not lead us to deny altogether the relevance of empirical strategies for social enquiry.

Here, Louch thinks Winch has been misled into thinking that

empirical knowledge (and thus empirical investigation) consists entirely of statistical or predictive statements. Louch's point is that the notion of empirical investigation should not be so narrowly conceived:

> it is a matter of empirical discovery that people can talk certain ways, for it is only in the context of the talk that we can claim to understand what they are doing and why they are doing it. So with my own variant of Winch's thesis. In morally explaining human practices the sociologist is not merely cloaking actions in the respectability of one's own moral convictions, but enriching the factual details so as to see what it is in the situation that could provide the agent with grounds for acting. (*op.cit.*, p. 175)

Thus, for Louch 'empirical discovery' through detailed observation and description is an irreducible component of social inquiry. Louch insists that although finding grounds for conduct seems to involve Winch's *a priori* notion of presenting arguments or offering moral judgements, the actual grounds available to social investigators 'consist in the events and circumstances which surround the investigated action', and, thus this is 'a matter of observation' (p. 176). The reestablishment of observation as the principal means whereby moral explanations for action are advanced has the effect of replacing the *a priorism* of Winch with a relativistic and empiricist mode of explanation. However, the loci and objects of explanation remain the same, forms of life, for example, a religious order or a military organisation as limned out by the participants' conceptions, reasons and attitudes or, in other words, the lived world of the rules and social relations which are constitutive of such forms of life.

It is, perhaps, this amended form of Winch's argument that has had a more pervasive influence (although largely unacknowledged) in social science since it is supportive of a role for empirical research and observational method which are central to the practice of the social sciences. Whilst Louch's insistence that we must attempt 'moral' explanations of social behaviour may be eyed with some suspicion, if not open hostility by some practitioners of social science, nonetheless, the idea that the social context of behaviour must play an important role in understanding the behaviour in question has very strong resonances within symbolic interactionist, ethnomethodological and phenomenological schools of thought.

In turn, it is these interpretive sociologies (including Weber's) that have presented realism with an explanatory problem; how to account for the interpretive moment of social reality within a reworked account of natural science. Realism accepts the whole framework of the humanist critique of positivism; the charge of naive objectivism, the correspondence theory of knowledge, its mechanistic conception of action, the need for *verstehen* forms of explanation, and so on. Above all it accepts the critique of 'reification' which is, according to the humanist approach, inscribed in the positivist version of social science. This critique, explicit in the humanist (interpretive) sociologies, but also implicit in the philosophical humanism of Winch and Louch, points to the dehumanisation of social forms by adducing external causal factors in their explanation. These causal factors in the positivist view are (according to the humanist interpretation of this view), supposedly *independent* of the social activities of individuals. They have a life and an influence of their own, and whilst their existence does not depend on the activities of individuals, the activities of individuals are in large part determined by those structures.

I want to argue that whilst in some respects the fear of reification has been justified in particular cases, the wholesale rejection of objectivist ontology that is contained in the humanist project was an overreaction which resulted in a solipsistic absorption into a self-sustaining interpretive universe. (Some of the more extreme and self-indulgent of these fads and fashions can be found in ethnomethodological work.) I would argue that this state of affairs resulted from several illicit equations. First, here was a conflation of forms of objectivism. Thus, it was contended that because naive objectivism was inadequate, therefore objectivism *per se* was inadequate. However, as I have indicated at various points in this book, the naive form of objectivism (correspondence, reification, mechanism, value-neutrality) can be distinguished from a more sophisticated version which does not possess any of these features.

In this sense objectivism refers to the existence of a social world as the products of human activity which, as *products* possess a *relative* autonomy from ongoing contemporaneous activity. Thus, this form of objectivism is predicated on the twin ideas of the productive nature of human activity, and the temporal and ontological distinction between the integrated consequences of past activity (intended or unintended) and the productive or reproductive effects of current activity. Formulated in this way objectivism does not propose a reified conception of social structure, but does preserve the notion of a social world external to, and parallel with, situated activity. Now this form of objectivism (and I shall spell out the finer details later in the discussion) does not repeat the pitfalls or inadequacies of the naive variety (correspondence, reification, mechanism, preinterpreted facts) but, nonetheless, was dispensed with along with the naive variety in the humanist critique of the supposedly reifying tendency of objectivism *per se*.

The other illicit equation that was imported into the interpretive critique by this overreaction to the perceived problem of reification was that between positivist naturalism and objectivism. Just as naive objectivism (was and is) taken to represent objectivism in general, so, too, objectivism was construed as synonymous with the naive version of naturalism which unthinkingly applied natural science methods to the study of social phenomena. There may be a case to be made that some forms of objectivist social theory do employ positivist forms of argument (for example, Durkheim and later structural functionalism) but it is incorrect to suggest thereby that all possible versions of objectivism are to be so identified. In other words it is possible to envisage a version of objectivism, like the one just outlined, that does not conform to the naive, positivist stereotype.

Thus, this neo-objectivism (as I shall call it from now on) does not view structural constraint as 'a source of causation more or less equivalent to the operation of impersonal causal forces in nature' (Giddens 1984, p. 174 but see Layder 1987 for a detailed critical commentary). The implication of this view is that objectivism is necessarily tied to a view of human behaviour as mechanically determined by external causal forces and in terms of which people have no choice; they are completely compelled by impersonal forces. Again, I will fill out the details of an alternative view later, but it is clear from what has already been said that the notion of the relative autonomy of structures commits this form of objectivism only to a form of reciprocal interdependence between situated social activity and its institutional (objective) context. It does not imply any lack of choice, or absolute determination. Importantly, it quite patently rejects the idea that objective features of social reality are anything like 'causal forces in nature'.

With reference to the above discussion it can be appreciated that the humanist/interpretive turn in social theory has been responsible for jettisoning both the flawed naive form of objectivism and the possibility of a more adequate sophisticated version. It is by means of an overreaction to the threatened obliteration of the 'freedom of action' of the human subject through reification that the humanist interpretive school has adopted an exclusively interpretive problematic as the epistemological basis of social science.

The realist problem with the humanist position was not its interpretive epistemology nor its ontological assumptions which radically rejected naive objectivism (and thus all forms of objectivism), but rather its eschewal of any form of natural science model as an exemplar for the social sciences. As realist naturalism is committed to notions of causality and causal processes in the social sciences and the identification of generative mechanisms and causal powers, the problem for realism was how to reconcile these concerns with the critique of objectivism and the endorsement of the interpretive moment that emerged from the humanist rejection of positivism.

In the next section I go on to suggest that many realist attempts to incorporate humanist insights into a reworked naturalism with its emphasis on causality have done so by somewhat crudely redefining humanist insights in causal terms. In so doing, they have incorporated the unargued rejection of an epistemologically adequate objectivism that is a central feature of humanism. Hence, they have been unable adequately to come to terms with the collective properties of social life in the form of a recognition of objectivist ontological components existing in tandem with interpretive aspects. This, of course, recalls my earlier argument about the importation of empiricist validity claims into realism via humanism. It is precisely the same mechanism that is at work here. The uncritical importation of the interpretive epistemological infrastructure effected an unacknowledged underlying link with an empiricist theory of knowledge that is shared by positivism and humanism.

PHENOMENOLOGICAL REALISM

One of the clearest examples of the unreflective 'tacking-on' of a realist concern with causal mechanisms to the basic humanist project of an interpretive epistemology and an anti-objectivist ontology can be seen in Harré's work (Harré 1979, 1981). Harré rejects the Humean notion of causality implicit in experimental psychology in that wherever there is a regular conjunction between events A and B such that B always follows event A then there is a causal relationship between the two with B being said to be caused by A. In this framework the 'subject' of the experiment is understood to be simply a transmitter or unreflective processor of information from the stimulus A which eventuates in the behavioural response B.

Quite naturally, Harré wants to reject the literal dehumanisation of the person (subject) involved in this behaviourist model. There is no genuine causal mechanism or locus of causal powers which has been invoked to explain the correlation between stimulus and response. Really there has been only a description of the correlation itself with the human individual simply acting as the passive mechanism of 'transmission' of the correlating relationship. According to the realist account we must treat the subjects of experiments 'as if' they were human beings, that is, beings endowed with intentionality, the ability to self-monitor their behaviour and to invest their environment with meaning and act on this basis. In short, the human agent must be seen as a spontaneous generator of behaviour in the social milieu rather then an empty vessel, a neutral medium through which information is conveyed.

In this sense, the individual is seen as the locus of powers to produce behaviour on the basis of meanings and the interpretation of cultural rules which may be more or less explicit. This view of the individual as a creative agent concentrates attention on linguistic performances in the elucidation of meaning and thus social actors accounts of their own behaviour become a crucial investigative focus. In fact it is really only the concern with the reconstructability of the meanings which actors ascribe to situations, through systematic investigations of the (restrospective) accounts that actors give of their behaviour in controlled interviews that distinguishes the content of 'ethogenics' (as this approach is called) from the substance of many of the humanistic disciplines to which I have already referred. Even here it could be argued that ethnomethodology overlaps considerably with ethogenics.

The distinguishing features at a formal level consist in the fact that the realist search for generative mechanisms in the explanation of behaviour identifies 'self-direction according to the meaning ascribed to the situation' (1972, *op.cit.*, p. 9) as the main causal mechanism. Thus, what is taken to be part of the theoretical context of symbolic interaction (Blumer 1967; Rock 1979), Winchian and Louchian social analysis, and which differentiates these humanist approaches from positivist naturalism, namely, the meaning-ascribing propensities of human individuals, becomes redefined and redescribed as a causal or generative mechanism. It is interesting to note that all the humanistic and existential (Sartre 1966) traditions of social analysis have stressed an anti-positivist concern with meaningful intentional action without the veneer of a natural science framework.

The issue here seems to be whether the notion of the self-generation of behaviour (through meaning-ascription) can be reappropriated as a form of causality. A further issue is, what is to be gained by relabelling this phenomenon as 'causal'? One convenient effect of the assertion self-direction according to meaning-ascription as the main causal mechanism is that it monopolises the territory of causal claims about social behaviour. Thus, social behaviour is exclusively self-directed and self-generated and cannot be the result of the effect of external (social structural) factors. In short, individuals are autonomous with respect to the environing forms of life in which they live out their lives.

This is precisely the exclusively personalist ontology that is claimed by the humanists of all persuasions. Thus, I have said, adequate versions of objectivism are eschewed along with naive versions. Harré is quite clear about this; he suggests that the notion of social structure as anything other than a rhetorical device used in actors' accounts is a fiction; a reification (1981). Here we see exactly the same overreaction to objectivism *per se* and a retreat into subjectivism. In this sense Harré's work occupies exactly the same terrain as ethnomethodology, which insists that structural concepts are of importance only if they enter into the actor's awareness. Thus 'power' as a structural resource has no existential status unless it figures in the consciousness of particular actors and thereby influences their behaviour (Benson 1974). These forms of subjectivism are reductionist and cannot theoretically or substantively explain or describe the constraints and enablements that forms of social organisation provide for actors as historical and institutional products of human activity (Layder 1981, 1985a).

The phenomenological empiricism of Harré's realism does not (and cannot) recognise the degree to which institutional conditions are sedimented in time and space and thus entailed in social relations of power and domination (Layder 1985, 1987). That is, it does not recognise the objective moment of social reality and its stratification or sedimentation in time and space. Any realism must recognise that the activity of individuals is variably related to these structural features, both in terms of the degree to which the activity itself is constrained and facilitated by these features, and by the degree to which this activity makes a difference to, or is transformative of, these features (Bordieu 1977; Layder 1981; Giddens 1984).

Realism cannot afford to understand the individual as the autonomous self-generator of his or her own behaviour. Such a position
leads to solipsicism, egocentrism and reductionism in relation to the
social context of behaviour. Realism must incorporate the idea that
individuals are more or less autonomous according to the social
circumstances which engender and define levels of autonomy in the
first place. These subjective and interpretive moments of social
reality have to be understood in the context of social organisational
conditions wherein the power to make a difference is reciprocally
related to these features of social reality. Objective conditions are
ontologically real in the sense that they exist independently of the
individual's perceptions and knowledgeability. That is, they have an
ontological constitution which is independent of cognising experience, but which the latter attempts to represent.

The attempt at representation in knowledge can take two forms.
First, there is the involved member(s) whose behaviour is under
scrutiny. Such members attempt to represent the social conditions
under which they operate in their perceptions, attitudes, commonsense and mutual (everyday) knowledge. Now whilst such mutual
knowledge may be fairly 'accurate' and adequate to the tasks at
hand and the problem of knowing 'how to go on' during routine
encounters, it would be a mistake to suppose that such knowledge
necessarily represents an accurate depiction of the technical, social
(discursive) circumstances which constitute the environment of their
activity.

Thus, the social scientist's attempt to represent the member's
world would involve two strands of analysis. First an attempt to
depict the locale *in terms of* the perceptions of members, and of
their mutual knowledge and so on; secondly, the analysis would
attempt a depiction of the technical and organisational structure and
the organisational interpenetrations which represent the backdrop of
social activities. It may be that an examination of mutual knowledge
will in some sense feed into the more technical description, but it
would be a mistake as in Harré's realism to fail to make a distinction
between phenomenological knowledge and technical knowledge of
objective conditions.

These are two senses in which the inability to incorporate objective
features of analysis contradicts two of the most often asserted axioms
of realism. First, it contradicts the notion of a world independent of
cognising experience, for in Harré's realism the notion of an objective world merely subserves or acts as a resource for members'

perceptions, reasons, and so on. The individual as a completely autonomous social agent simply 'apprehends' the objective world without constraint. Thus, social reality has no properties of its own and social analysis is reduced to a methodological individualism. The notion of an independent world is collapsed into members' accounts and is deemed to be a figment of members' imaginations. This leads to the second point in that Harré here seems to discount the veracity of members' accounts. Thus, when they invoke social structural factors as part of their explanations or accounts, they are deemed by Harré to have no real substance; they are fictions, merely rhetorical devices. Perhaps realism should heed its own advice and take seriously members' awareness and apprehensions of the objective structures and conditions which transcend their experience.

An empirical example may serve to illustrate the idea that objective social conditions have a relatively independent role to play in social investigation but that this does not discount members' meanings, reasons, mutual knowledge and the like; it merely underlines the complementarity and reciprocal influence of these different ontological domains of the social. I will draw upon my own research into (dramatic) actors and the acting profession (Layder 1981, 1984). My main point here is that to focus exclusively on dramatic actors' reasons or accounts of their career experiences will produce no systematic knowledge of the contextual conditions (in this case the structure of the labour market) which partly produce those experiences. Thus, in acting the internal labour market is hierarchically segmented and the contractual basis of work is short-term (for the run-of-the show in live theatre, or for the duration of a project/engagement in the mechanical media). Access to work in general and the best acting jobs in particular, is distributed unevenly between the segments, the 'outer circle' (15 per cent) and the élite (5 per cent) taking by far the major share, whilst the mass (80 per cent) are unemployed (in acting, although they may do 'temporary' work) for most of the time. This uneven access to work opportunities is reproduced and reinforced by the work practices and the interrelationships between casting directors (who filter most of the work) and the top theatrical agents (personal managers).

Actors may either be totally unaware or only dimly and vaguely aware of the structure of the labour market in which they live out their occupational lives and the mechanisms which reproduce it. This is not to say that actors' 'reasons' for, and the accounts of, their behaviour do not tell us anything about careers in acting. Indeed much valuable information on these subjective and intersubjective aspects of acting careers, such as alienation and powerlessness, styles of interaction, or types of involvement and commitment, may be gleaned in this way. However, one cannot infer from these subjective and interactive accounts the structural, contextual conditions (the internal labour market and so forth) which shape actors' careers. To a certain extent dramatic actors (and social actors in general) are knowledgeable and reflexively intentional about the workaday 'conditions' to which they are subject (for instance, the rehearsal schedules, the acting 'skills' required of them, the 'grapevine' of job information, and so on), but to say this is not the same thing as claiming that they know about the contextual conditions as described above. Thus also, to claim that intentionality, reflexiveness, interaction are partly constrained by these conditions is not to posit a mechanically deterministic theory of behaviour (as in positivism, behaviourism, structural determinism and so forth) but merely to recognise the generative power of the social structures and conditions that provide the context for these individual and interactive experiences. This is the point at which an exclusive ontology of 'reason' explanations, that is, the identification of explanations in social science as being concordant with the meanings, accounts or commonsense understandings of those being studied, represents an exaggerated claim on validity, and an arbitrary delineation of theoretical explanation.

Realism must draw on traditions of social analysis which emphasise the collectivist and objectivist moments of social reality as well as the individualist or subjectivist moments. Epistemologically, this means not simply accepting phenomenological empiricism and a personalist ontology (Roche 1973) as the easy alternative to orthodox positivism, but rather, it means adopting a form of realism which can accommodate the collectivist or objectivised moments of social reality.

EPISTEMOLOGY AND THE CONCEPT OF SOCIAL RELATION

If phenomenological realism tends to reproduce the epistemological and ontological presuppositions of philosophical humanism, Bhaskar (1979) most definitely attempts to avoid this by mounting a sustained attack on both methodological individualism in sociology (pp. 34–9) and Winch's hermeneutics (pp. 169–95). Methodological individualism presupposes a flat ontology of individuals and insists that facts about social phenomena can be explained solely in term of facts about individuals. Bhaskar's model of 'transformative activity' rejects this and asserts the centrality of the ontological distinction between people and societies. Also, whilst conceding that there is an important interpretive moment to social analysis, Bhaskar rejects Winch's idea that this exhausts the possibilities of social analysis; 'Social Science is not only concerned with actions, it is concerned with their conditions and consequences (including the states and relations of structures and agents)' (p. 180).

Now in so far as Bhaskar's schema makes a radical departure from the presuppositions of humanism and attempts to fashion a theoretical dialogue between interpretive and macro-structural approaches in sociology then I am very much in agreement. However, despite the overall agreement about objectives (and some of the analytic means of achieving these) there are some features of Bhaskar's argument which are either ambiguous or seem to lack the theoretical wherewithal to support entirely the objective he undertakes to achieve.

First, as I mentioned in chapter 3, I think it is a mistake to posit ontological privilege over and against epistemological matters. I showed in chapter 3 that such a posture assumes that ontological factors are uncontaminated by the very mediation of frames of meaning that is the *raison d'être* of hermeneutics. In this case the assertion of ontological privilege leaves out of account the constructional role that prior theoretical discourses (and their interweaving) play in the establishment of ontological models. The role of epistemological and theoretical assumptions is of paramount importance and cannot be underestimated. It is precisely Bhaskar's silence on this matter that prevents him from reconciling the conflicting insights of empiricism and rationalism in the manner that he supposes. The overriding of epistemological concerns (the same applies to Giddens) by the assertion of ontological privilege is a major means whereby empiricism is allowed to leak unchecked into the whole realist framework. The assumed pristine giveness of Bhaskar's 'irreducible ontological features' of social reality completely mutes the role of rationalist elements in the knowledge process. Thus, empiricism is not reconciled with rationalism, the former is simply endorsed (if only implicitly) by the assertion of ontological privilege. This is not the only source of an empiricist leakage which threatens to flood Bhaskar's framework.

The submerging of epistemological matters has ramifications for Bhaskar's attempt to theoretically underwrite the notion of the social conditions of action, and with which he wants to oppose Winch's idea that social analysis is solely about the interpretation of action. However, here again we have Bhaskar making another ontological claim, that there is an irreducible material dimension to social reality which gives rise to material conditions of action. Social reality is thus more than linguistically constituted as Winch would have it. However, Bhaskar does not pinpoint an epistemological position which would accommodate this claim; he simply assumes it to be the case. Thus, he does not avail himself of the opportunity of establishing the epistemological preconditions of the objectivist moment contained in the notion of social conditions. This is more clearly emphasised in his conception of 'social relation'.

The concept of social relation is pivotal to Bhaskar's definition of the subject matter of sociology. This latter is not as the methodological individualists would have it, the study of individuals, nor is it primarily the study of collective phenomena like riots or groups. Rather, sociology is concerned with 'the persistent *relations* between individuals (and groups)' and such relations are 'general and relatively enduring' (p. 36). Now, this formal version looks very attractive. It seems to offer the possibility of producing the other half of the epistemological equation that realism needs to balance the interpretive/empiricist component. However, because of Bhaskar's concentration on the description of irreducible ontological features, this epistemological support never materialises. Thus, he operates with a definition of 'social relation' which does not call upon objectivist epistemology (the sophisticated version), but relies entirely on the empiricist idea of 'social relations' as concrete relation*ships* between actual actors.

> In social life only relations endure. Note also that such relations include relationships between people and nature and social products (such as machines and firms) *as well as interpersonal ones.* (my emphasis) (p. 52)

Bhaskar goes on to say that this relational conception allows one to focus on a range of questions having to do with the distribution of the structural conditions of action and the differential allocation of resources (of all kinds). As a consequence, this allows one to situate the possibility of antagonistic interest groups in society. It is precisely these kinds of questions that one would want a realist social science to address since they are important questions. However, the ability to focus on such a range of questions *does not* and *cannot* follow from the definition of social relation that Bhaskar offers us. Since Bhaskar conflates a *potentially objectivist* notion of social relation with the orthodox empiricist conception of social *relationship*, his ability to address questions about the structural distribution of conditions of action is thwarted by taking this conceptual route. In this respect Bhaskar simply jumps levels of analysis because his conceptual framework does not permit the transition.

One cannot inquire about the conditions of action by proposing a conception of 'social relation' which addresses the interiority of concrete relationships in an empiricist sense. One has to call upon some kind of objectivist epistemology to be able to address the very different ontological domain of the conditions of action. In this respect Bhaskar's conception is very like that of Giddens (1984) where he suggests that social relations can be conceptualised as a *given* presence/absence of actors and their time-space pathways, where these latter are supposedly 'influenced by basic institutional parameters'. Since Giddens' schema possesses the same underlying inadequacies as Bhaskar's let me concentrate for a moment on Giddens' work. Generally the point is the same, that both Bhaskar's and Giddens' notions of social relation are entirely empiricist, that is, given, and, actual or potential/absent relationships between concrete actors tell us nothing about the way *reproduced* social relations (as reflected in 'basic institutional parameters') actually *do* influence the regionalised time-space pathways of situated individuals.

To fit in with his presence/absence schema, Giddens defines social relations as both concrete relations between situated actors (social integration), and absent or potential relations between actors projected into time-space (system integration), and while both of these are, according to Giddens, influenced by 'basic institutional parameters', these remain untheorised or unexplained in his characterisation of the connection between social and system integration. The theorisation of the influence of institutional parameters is dissolved into a description of the connection between social and system integration as 'members' time-space paths'.

There is no sense here in which social relations can be understood as reproduced allocative and authoritative resources which are not themselves the concrete (or potential) relationships between actual actors, but rather, the social conditions under which the concrete relations and time-space paths of actors are constituted in the first place. Here, 'social relation' refers to the preconstituted social constraints and facilities that institutional features represent precisely because they have been stretched in time and space through a historical process of social reproduction. This sense of 'social relation' goes beyond the empiricist limitations of the notion of concrete relationships between two or more actors (as found in Weber 1964), and posits unobservable structural mechanisms (Keat and Urry 1975) which underlie and produce these observable relationships or action pathways of societal members.

These unobservable structural mechanisms are, in other words, the social conditions of existence of both the concrete relations that human agents make with each other in empirical terms, and the interactional interchanges that result from these. This is why it is worth preserving a distinction between the concept of social *relation* as referring to reproduced institutional properties, and social *relationship* which refers to concrete relationships between describable actors. Again, this distinction refers to, and is reflective of, different ontological features present in social reality.

The lack of an ontological distinction is implicit in the concept of social relation in both the work of Bhaskar and Giddens, and the absence or rejection of any objectivist epistemological support for this (Giddens rejects objectivism *per se*), leaves their conceptual frameworks unable to theorise human agency as constrained and generally influenced by pre-existing asymmetrical structural relations of power (control over of resources) as opposed to the given powers of concrete individuals (Layder 1985a). Such power relations are neutralised in the continuous and 'even' ontological presence/-absence of concrete relationships between actors and their projected pathways through time and space. The dualistic position which I advocate here, requires us to recognise two senses in which 'stretching' occurs in social-relational terms. First, it has to be considered in terms of the stretching of social relation*ships* in empiricist terms, that is, the sense in which Giddens projects the relationships between actors in situations of co-presence into absent but potential 'connections between those who are physically absent in time or space' (1984, p. 28). Second, in the realist or objectivist sense in which reproduced social relations of an allocative and authoritative kind, such as is reflected by different institutional contexts, are stretched over time and space and are implicated in social activity in specific situated contexts.

The stretching in this latter sense is not carried by or traced in, the action pathways of individuals in their day-to-day activities; rather, it is inscribed in institutional contexts considered as the ontologically distinct and relatively independent (structural) conditions of behaviour. Thus, this stretching cannot be measured in the rather loose and neutral terms that Giddens proposes, namely, regionalised time-space pathways; rather it has to be measured in terms of scope, domains of influence, and connectedness of particular structural parameters. In terms of these criteria, reproduced social relations stretch *forward* and *backward* in time and space in relation to specific empirical instances of social activity.

Consider, for example, the case of an encounter between workers, foremen and management on the factory floor. In this context of co-presence reproduced institutional constraints and enablements can be understood to stretch forwards and backwards in time and space to condition the concrete interactional exchanges in the encounter. Thus, the situation of co-presence operates at, and is influenced by, different levels of social reality. First, it operates in terms of the immediacy of the encounter itself and the actual relationships between the interactants, including their respective personalities and their personal powers. It also involves the immediate issue that brings them together namely, is it merely a friendly encounter during work time, or is it a situation in which someone is being disciplined, or is it a prelude to union-management negotiations? The immediacy of the encounter also involves Giddens' idea of the routinised and regionalised pathways through, in this case, organisational space and time, and the points of intersection or connection that exist between the people involved. It also includes the idea that past encounters between the same people will have a 'knock-on' or spillover effect on the present encounter.

However, at the same time, the situation of co-presence is being influenced and conditioned by the seemingly more remote relations of autonomy and dependence which characterise capital-labour relations (Krekel 1980). From the viewpoint of this specific encounter, social relations in the latter sense are stretched both forwards and backwards in time and space. It is because relations of co-presence themselves always reach forward into a future of extended space-time that this anticipated future is conditioned by a horizon of authoritative relations between labour and capital considered in terms of collective properties and resources. The anticipated future horizon of autonomy and dependence operates independently of, but also conditions, the spillover or 'knock-on' effect of situated encounters described previously.

At the same time, these reproduced social relations stretch backwards in time and space in so far as this anticipated future horizon is predicated on the continuing existence of collective relations of domination and subordination which have emerged through an historical process (Edwards 1979; Braverman 1974), involving the transformative activity of human agents. That is, capital/labour relations are presently constituted, and as an anticipated future state of affairs, have been decisively influenced by the reproductive and transformative activity of human agents in the historical past.

From an analytic point of view, this backwards and forwards stretching cuts across the binary line between the properties of situational reality (including personal attributes in so far as these affect the construction of situational reality), and the negotiated 'emergents' (Blumer 1969; Garfinkel 1967), and collective institutional properties that emerge from the historical fashioning of relations of domination and subordination between social groupings (Edwards 1979; Burawoy 1979). Analytically, we can say there is a constant 'switching' between these two levels of reality as situated activity unfolds over time. I stress the word 'analytically' because from the point of view of the individuals caught up in the unfolding reality of situational encounters nothing of this sort seems to occur. From the point of view of the involved participant, encounters are experienced as an 'even presence' (albeit one which has a history and a future). The member, the experiencer who has to cut a swathe through social time and space (Giddens' regionalised pathways) generally does not sense any bridgeheads between these two aspects of social reality, not the least because they extend beyond an empiricist ontology of sensorily apprehensible phenomena. In any case, such perceptual or cognitive recognition is not a prerequisite for knowing 'how to go on' in social encounters, or for solving the more pressing practical problems of getting along with one's fellow human beings.

I have suggested that both Bhaskar's and Giddens' conceptions of social relations are unimodal and based on the empiricist notion of concrete relationships between actual actors, rather than an attempt to depict the ontologically distinct conditions of action. Irrespective of the inadequacies of such a position for social analysis in general (Layder 1987; Barbalet 1987) in Giddens case this is entirely consonant with his avowed rejection of any form of objectivism, by which he means a theoretical position which conceptualises social structural phenomena as (relatively) independent of actors' motives and reasons. (1984, p. 181).

In Bhaskar's case the position is more ambiguous. He speaks freely of the social conditions of action *as if* they were ontologically distinct phenomena but nowhere states an objectivist epistemological position which would support this. He speaks of the idea that the relational nature of the subject matter of sociology *enables* one to ask questions about the social conditions of action and the distribution of resources, but, as we have seen, this conception of social relations could not uphold this claim. He also speaks of social structures as *already made*, and as ontologically distinct from people, although again he nowhere calls upon objectivist explanatory forms to buttress his claim. It seems that Bhaskar in some respects is happy to entertain the idea of objectivist moments of social reality but either refrains from explicitly formulating this idea or, alternatively, the concepts he produces, like that of 'social relation', fail to underwrite the broader claims of his analysis. I want now to pursue some further implications of the above issues in relation to Bhaskar's model of social ontology as a whole.

SOCIAL ONTOLOGY: AN EXTENDED STRATIFIED VIEW

Bhaskar situates his 'transformational model of the society/person connection' in the context of three alternative models. The first, which sees social objects 'as the results of (or as constituted by), intentional or meaningful human behaviour' (1979, pp. 39–40), is, according to Bhaskar, represented by Weber. The second, represented by Durkheim, sees social objects 'as possessing a life of their own, external to and coercing the individual' (1979, pp. 39–40). All schools of social thought, phenomenology, existentialism, functionalism, structuralism and the different varieties of Marxism, can be seen as instances of one or more of these positions. The most pressing problem for social theory is to find some alternative model which combines both the individual and collective aspects of social reality which are falsely separated in these opposing forms of reductionism.

Bhaskar points out that Berger and Luckmann (1967) have already attempted to do this with a 'dialectical' model wherein society forms or produces the individuals who create society and these individuals in turn produce society in a continuous dialectical process 'composed of the three moments of externalization, objectivation and internalization' (1967, p. 147). Bhaskar quickly rejects this model on the grounds that in seeking to avoid the errors of the other two models, it only succeeds in combining them. As Bhaskar puts it; 'it encourages on the one hand a voluntaristic idealism with respect to our understanding of social structure and on the other, a mechanistic determinism with respect to our understanding of people' (1979, p. 42).

Bhaskar insists that societies and people cannot be understood as different moments of the same process as in the dialectical model; rather, they must be understood as ontologically distinct phenomena. I do not feel that this two-fold characterisation of social reality goes far enough; and I shall trace out the implications of this further on. However, for the moment let us agree with Bhaskar that people and society refer to radically different kinds of things. How do they differ? Let us take societies first. Here, Bhaskar incorporates Durkheim's (1982) ideas on the properties of social facts. Thus, it is the ready-made character of social phenomena such as beliefs and practices, language structure and so forth, that is, their existence prior to the birth of the individuals who utilise them in their social activity which confers on them their exterior and coercive power. Social structure in short, is already made and thus people in their social activities do not create society (as in the Weberian and dialectical models); rather, they reproduce or transform it. As Bhaskar puts it 'conscious human activity consists in work on given objects' (1979, p. 42). For example, people cannot communicate with each other without utilising existing media, such as the language and linguistic style of the social grouping to which they belong.

However, Bhaskar stresses that we must be careful not to reify society (as does Durkheim) since society would not exist without human activity, and this activity itself would not exist unless human agents had a conception of what they were doing. Thus, social structures (unlike natural structures) are dependent upon the activities they govern and the agents' conceptions of what they are doing. However, I would argue that this idea erodes the notion that structures are ontologically distinct in the sense of being *already made;* that they are the conditions of intentional activity. How can social structures be the prior conditions of human agency at the same time as being dependent upon this same agency for their very existence?

It would be better to say that structures are concept and activity-*connected* (rather than dependent), since structures, if they are already made, must have a relative autonomy from situated activity, and thus cannot be said to be activity- (or concept-) dependent. It is situated activity itself which is more accurately described as concept- and activity-dependent (see further on). Here, it seems that Bhaskar has conflated the institutional (structural) and the situational levels of social reality and the effects of transformative activity at these different levels. In so doing Bhaskar has misleadingly compacted all these elements into the same time-space.

Although Bhaskar's notion of structure attempts to represent the conditions of agency, it does not *determine* agency in a mechanical fashion. Thus, the ontological properties of people, such as their intentionality and their ability to monitor their own performances are such that they are able to 'work on' the conditions which impose limits on their activity and create their own areas of freedom within these limits. For Bhaskar, this formulation 'preserves the status of human agency while doing away with the myth of creation' (1979, p. 45). In this sense subjects transform as well as reproduce the social structural conditions under which they act.

Thus, both society (structures) and human praxis possess a dual character:

> Society is both the ever-present *condition* (material cause) and the continually reproduced *outcome* of human agency. And praxis is both work, that is, conscious *production*, and (normally unconscious) *reproduction* of the conditions of production, that is society. (1979, p. 44)

The previously mentioned tension recurs here, in the sense that while society is both the condition and the reproduced outcome of human agency, to say that praxis is not only the reproduction but also the production of its own conditions (that is, structure), seems to resurrect rather than abolish the myth of creation. How else can we understand the phrase 'the production of the conditions of human agency' other than in the sense of 'creating' these conditions.

I would argue that there is *a sense* in which social reproduction is at the same time a productive process in that it involves human work on given social objects such as cultural rules and the employment of interpretive schemes and so on, but this is patently not the same thing as saying that this is production of the conditions of production. This formulation over-simplifies the issues involved, and confuses the generic notions of 'agency', 'transformative activity' and 'social production' in an abstract sense with the more particular concrete notions involved in actual instances of the situated conduct of describable actors.

I want to develop an alternative schema to Bhaskar's. To do this I want to address three central issues relating to this model which, in my view, also represent its major weaknesses. These are first, the conflating of important ontological elements of social reality. I shall argue that these should be unpacked and carefully distinguished in order to understand the different modes and levels of transformative activity. Second, a major feature of this revised ontology must incorporate the notion that the structural properties of society possess a relative independence from the social activities which they condition. Third, the compacting of temporal (and spatial) referents must be reversed and remodelled to assimilate the ontological features mentioned above. In particular the one-dimensional view of time implicit in the schema must give way to a multi-dimensional view.

Bhaskar's simple twofold distinction between people and society/social structure conflates a number of social phenomena which must be distinguished in terms of their ontological properties. First, the dichotomy does not distinguish between individual and collective *actors* or agents who are responsible for transformative activity. Second, Bhaskar's schema does not distinguish different *contexts* which condition social activity; that is, situational and structural contexts (see Figure 5.1).

As regards types of actor or agency, it is of paramount importance to distinguish between the transformative potential of individuals as a result of their intentionality, purposiveness, interpretive abilities and so forth, and the transformative potential of various collective forms of agency. Although the distinction between individual and collective agency is not always capable of exact definition there is, nonetheless, a significant difference between small-scale focussed interactions and larger collective phenomena. In a focussed gathering (interaction in a coffee bar, private party or the like) any *one* individual involved is able to orient themselves towards the behaviour of any of the others, and thus, their own behaviour is thereby influenced, as well as influential. By contrast, with larger-scale collective phenomena focal individuals are no longer simply influenced by the behaviour of other significant individuals, but by the collectivity as a whole. Also, the products of collective agency (an urban riot, a legal enact-

Ontological Feature	Properties
TYPE OF ACTOR	
Persons (Individual)	Intentionality, purposiveness, reflexive monitoring, interpretive skills Biographical time
Collectivities (Inchoate or Organised)	Common interests, collective decision-making, action and 'definitions' Group or Organisational Time
TYPE OF CONTEXT	
Situations (One-off encounters, sequential or discontinuous episodes)	Emergent features of face-to-face interaction, for instance, 'definitions' of reality, and indexicality of meaning Indexical time
Structures (power relations and distributions of resources)	Institutional constraints and enablements mediated by authoritative, allocative and cultural resources (Third World phenomena) Institutional Time

FIGURE 5.1 *A Stratified Ontology of the Social*

ment enforced by a pressure group, and so on) far exceed the transformative capacities of small gatherings of individuals.

It is clear that collective phenomena are multifarious – consider the differences between street gangs, crowds at sporting events, spontaneous uprisings, theatre or cinema audiences, social classes considered as historical actors, formally organised groupings such as trade unions, professional associations or employers associations; however, I do not propose to make any detailed analysis of the distinctions between such phenomena. It suffices for present purposes to emphasise the principal distinction between individual and collective actors in terms of whether the interaction is small-scale and focussed or not, and the consequent capability of individuals to formulate their own behaviour by monitoring the behaviour of (all) the other individuals involved. Of course, the question of the time-scale and spatial referents concerned are also important here; as, for example, the difference between a focussed interaction in a coffee bar, and working class struggles to achieve political and welfare rights so vividly highlights.

The distinction between individual and collective forms of agency are missing in Bhaskar's account. His model treats agency as unimodal and thus the transformative effects of individual and collective actors are treated identically. Furthermore, their transformative effects are compacted into one-dimensional time and space.

This is exacerbated by a concomitant lack of distinction between two principal types of social context which condition individual and collective social activity. Whilst Bhaskar is concerned with the process of social production and reproduction, he makes no attempt to analyse the role of the situational context in these processes. By contrast, writers from quite different theoretical traditions have often recognised the significance of situated behaviour but have failed to analyse its implications for the production and reproduction of structure, generally because they reject an ontological distinction between structures and people and/or social activity (see Blumer 1969; Becker 1970). These writers fear that such ontological distinctions represent reifications of social reality which have to be avoided at all costs (Rock 1979). However, Bhaskar believes that reification is avoided if structures are conceptualised as activity- and concept-dependent. I would go further and argue that to accord social structures a relative independence from the activities they condition does not necessarily entail reification.

So although Bhaskar concerns himself with the production and reproduction of structure, the situated character of social activity is accorded no particular importance in his schema. However, it is clear as interactionists and phenomenologists have shown, that the interactional emergents of situated encounters (ranging from one-off, transient encounters, to the more routine elements of social organisation, for example, between family members or hospital personnel) are significant elements affecting both the unfolding of present activity and the patterning of further encounters in the future. I believe it is important to draw out the implications of these interactional emergents for the production and reproduction of structure.

In so far as the situated character of behaviour involves the actual conduct of describable actors, then in principle, both individual (focussed) and collective forms of agency may be situated. However, most analyses of situated interaction have concentrated on the dynamics and emergents of small-scale focussed interactions, and thus the following comments are more pertinent to them. The type of interactional emergents that have been highlighted particularly in the work of symbolic interactionists is the creation and/or negotiation of meaning (Mead 1967; Blumer 1969), and thus of 'definitions' of the situation. Notwithstanding the criticism that often meanings and definitions are externally imposed on situations by various powerful groups, nonetheless there is enough evidence to support the idea that a certain amount of negotiation of meaning or situational definition takes place amongst participants in situated interaction (Laing and Esterson 1964; Glaser and Strauss 1965).

It is with reference to the purely situated aspects of behaviour that Bhaskar's dictum about the activity- and concept-dependence of social structures holds most sway. (Although it is here that situated activity becomes conflated with the concept of social structure in Bhaskar's schema.) Thus, situated behaviour is activity and concept dependent in the sense that the activity itself only remains in existence during the continued presence of particular people in particular circumstances. Once the participants disperse themselves in time and space, then the emergent conceptions, perceptions and activities bound up with the particular situation largely evaporate. In this sense, the emergent properties of situations only exist, to use Bhaskar's phraseology, in virtue of the activities they govern.

However, it is also clear that the situational context is not completely autonomous with regard to its effects on behaviour; it is itself enveloped by a broader structural context. This is the point at which the properties of social structures are ontologically distinguishable from situated activity. Social structures, such as economic and social institutions, value and cultural systems, have a *relative* autonomy from the situated activity which they in part govern. Thus, although any social structure depends upon the existence of situated activity *in a generic sense* (that is, without some human agents reproducing its features there would be no structure), they do *not* depend on this or that specific episode of situated activity.

For example, the role expectations associated with parenthood influence, but do not determine, this or that person's specific behaviour as a parent, and although instances of situated behaviour do represent instantiations of structure in this sense, they do not thereby arbitrate the continuance of the structure or its effects. The distinction between the generic and the specific senses of the notion of situated activity is a very important one here. The absence of such a distinction in the work of Bhaskar and other realists partly explains why they fail to grasp the importance of an objectivist epistemological component in the notion of the relative autonomy of structures and the distinctiveness of situated activity. It also masks the different levels and time scales of social reality in which productive and reproductive activity takes place.

The relative autonomy of structures does not undermine the fact that they are always the creations of historically located human activity (transformative activity). As human creations, they are also susceptible to alteration, transformation or even eradication at the hands of human actors. However, the rejection of the idea of the complete permanence of structures should not lead us to the equally erroneous assumption that they are continually being modified or 'recreated' by the everyday activities of the people who are subject to their influence (as in Giddens 1976, 1981).

It also has to be recognised that the degree of durability of social structures is variable; some social structures are more obdurate than others. The degree to which social structures are resistant to change depends not only on how sedimented they are in time and space (Giddens 1984), and the nature of their properties but also on the extent to which they are penetrated by relations of power based on the collective monopolisation of authoritative and distributive resources, and the control of access to these resources (see Layder 1985a). Forms of power relation (relations of domination and subordination) are an intrinsic feature of structures, and thus it could be said that such power is instanciated in structure just as much as it is instanciated in action (see Lukes 1977, and Giddens 1979 for a one-dimensional 'action' view of power). The nature of the relations of domination and subordination between social groups affects the degree of resistance that social structures offer to both internal and external pressures for change.

Characterised in this way, structures are the preformed pattern of social relations historically created and reproduced over time by human agency that individuals are socialised into at birth, and which continue to confront them as future constraints on their activity. Again, such structures may be 'in process' or changing through time (at variable rates according to the specific circumstances surrounding them), as the result of human activity. The point is that such transformative activity is constrained and conditioned by the structures that it has to confront as established relations of power. All transformative activity has to 'work on', and thus has to be structured by (already) reproduced social relations. Similarly, although particular structures may change fundamentally or even disappear over time (for example, changes in the social organisation of particular occupations and labour markets), at any particular point in time society as a whole is composed of concatenations of such structures that have been reproduced through human activity and which continue to change at different rates.

Structures are not only concerned with the delimitation of behaviour/activity, nor is the qualified determinism involved in the notion of constraint to be confused with the idea of the *complete* structural determination of agency which appears in the work of some structuralists, particularly of a Marxist persuasion (Althusser 1969). The confusion of these two forms of determinism, one limited and relative, the other complete and closed, is a feature of the writing of several theorists who have criticised and rejected all forms of objectivist modes of analysis (see, for example, Lukes 1977; Giddens 1984).

Thus, this conception of structure is two-sided, providing *both* constraints and enablements with respect to social activity. Thus, speaking a particular language not only limits the user's expressive range through the mandatory use of grammatical, syntactical and lexical forms, but also provides the speaker with a fund of symbols and communicative resources with which to express a multiplicity of unique sentences and meanings. Also, the objectivist notion of constraint insists that constraints exist in a double sense. First, as external and independently constituted 'obstacles' to the achievement of socially defined statuses. Second, constraints exist in terms of the subjective orientations of individuals towards these objective constraints, and nearly always allow some element of choice.

This, of course, carries the implication that if the actor rejects the constraint then he or she will have to forgo automatically the benefits, 'rewards' or objectives associated with actually taking the constraint into account. Entry into an occupational group provides a good example of the constraints that function as obstacles to entry. The potential member has to meet certain 'requirements' (experience, accreditation, sponsorship and the like), before being allowed entrance. Similarly, movements up occupational hierarchies require that the individual goes 'through the hoops' of organised appraisals and meets the criteria laid down in them, before élite positions can be reached (Sofer 1970). In emphasising the actor's strategic orientation to constraints I am not suggesting that this is the same thing as the 'interpretation' of constraints. This latter is a corollary of intentionality and indeed represents a person's recreations of structure within situations which the general process of social reproduction necessarily entails.

Now let me trace out the implications of this ontological schema for a reworked account of the processes of production and reproduction. First, there are two main ontological domains or contexts in which these processes are worked out. In reality these domains (situational and structural) overlap and interpenetrate each other, but nonetheless they have quite different properties. These properties relate to their relative durability and dispersal in time and space and their degree of resistance to, or propensity for, transformation. In tandem with these contexts, there are two principal modes of agency (individual and collective) which generate transformations or replications of these different aspects of social reality. Processes of production and reproduction at the situational level must not be confused with structural transformation or replication, and similarly, individual contributions to (local) reality constructions must not be confused with collective transformations of institutional structures.

As I have said, these distinctions are conditioned by the central notions of durability, and dispersal in time and space. Thus, the different modes of agency and their principal domains or contexts are marked out by their different temporal and spatial referents. Individuals are characterised by the temporal and spatial sequencing of their biographical careers. Collective actors are clearly not solely governed by the biographical careers of their constituent individuals and depend more on the longevity of the group considered as a whole (there are, of course, vast differences between crowds and trade unions in terms of durability and dispersal). Situated contexts of activity are in a sense governed by indexical time and depend upon the participation and engagement of specific describable actors. There is a tendency for the local reality constructions engendered by situated interactions to vanish or evaporate when the constituent actors disperse themselves. However, some constructions achieve a relative durability in that they are recreated in subsequent encounters with the same participants (as is exemplified in workers' 'games' (Burawoy 1979), or work routines (Layder 1981).

However, it is clear that situated activity represents the 'surface time' of socio-cultural localities which are amenable to renegotiation in routine or everyday encounters. Structures, by contrast, represent institutional time which is governed by a number of factors, such as the degree of (already-achieved) sedimentation in the cultural habits and resources of a community, the nature of their properties (compare gender distinctions with bureaucracy), and their penetration by social relations of power. All of these add up to the variable durability and malleability of structures when we compare them with other structures, although this institutional sedimentation marks them off from the more evanescent and volatile renegotiations which characterise situated activity.

All these modalities and calibrations of time (biographical, group, situational and structural) interact with the various ontological properties of agency and context (dispersal, size, durability and so on), to produce different effects on production and reproduction. That is, the effects of these temporal modalities on the transformative or replicative potential of agency are differentially distributed, not conflated as they are in Bhaskar's schema.

CONCLUSION

In this chapter I began by tracing the humanist antecedents of some of the elements that are still present in realist explanations of social behaviour. This has led to a species of phenomenological realism which has reproduced the same inadequacies as humanism with reference both to its explanatory base and its ontological presuppositions. I have also argued that the more sophisticated forms of realism, which attempt to include *as well as* go beyond the phenomenological level to embrace ontologically distinct social structural forms, have been hampered by residual attachments to humanist elements. In this respect I have attempted to shore-up and reformulate some of the epistemological and ontological elements and characterisations that stand in the way of adequate representation in a realist conception of social science.

6 The Language of Social Analysis

THE RELATION BETWEEN LAY AND SOCIAL SCIENTIFIC LANGUAGE

In previous chapters, particularly the last, I argued that the humanist challenge to positivism had the effect of leaving problematic residual imprints on the realist project as a result of realism's attempt to embrace the insights of humanism. In this chapter I want to extend this line of thought into a discussion of the role of language in social scientific analysis, particularly as this concerns the question of the relation between theory and evidence. My argument is that a realist conception of social science must clearly reject the humanist characterisation of the relation between lay and social scientific terms. Furthermore, I argue that this is a necessary prerequisite to an adequate understanding of the relation between theory and evidence; that is, one which is able to embrace both the stratified nature of social reality and the various discourses of social science as I have described them previously.

With this objective in mind I wish to concentrate on one specific characterisation of the relation between lay and social scientific language; Giddens' notion of a 'slippage' or interchange between the two sorts of language. In this respect I view Giddens' model as the most sophisticated examplar of a humanist position on this question. Ultimately, however, I argue that Giddens' model is over-generalised and does not distinguish sufficiently between types of language and levels of analysis in social science. Thus, I present an alternative model which more adequately deals with these features.

Giddens' own position draws upon the ideas of Schutz and Winch, but emends them and goes beyond them to fashion a distinct viewpoint. In this sense Giddens' more elaborate position subsumes that of Schutz and Winch. Also, Giddens' position has definite affinities with other humanist positions (not withstanding the differences within humanism). Thus, as a prelude to the discussion of Giddens' ideas I want to focus on a loosely formed humanist 'orthodoxy' (about the relation between lay and social scientific language) which Giddens' position subsumes.

After presenting an alternative model of the relation between lay and social scientific language, the second part of this chapter turns more directly to the question of the relation between theory and evidence in social research. In particular, it spotlights the issue of conceptual innovation in qualitative research. As I pointed out in chapter 3, qualitative research has been a primary focus of interest when realists have broached the question of 'alternative' methods or approaches to research.

However, I argue here that qualitative research raises the question of the relationship between macro and micro levels of analysis and the associated issue of the types of concepts and language that are appropriate to each level. Realists have talked loosely about the potential of qualitative research either without attending to these problems, or they have assumed that macro features are simply aggregations of micro features. In chapter 5 and the present one, I make it plain that although macro and micro features are implicated in each other, they possess ontologically distinct properties. Any characterisation of the relation between theory (or concepts) and the evidence revealed and collected in and through qualitative research must be able to account for, and do justice to, these properties.

HUMANISM AND THE INTERCHANGE MODEL

Humanism has tended to erode the distinction between lay language and that of social science by suggesting that in principle both are grounded in the vicissitudes of everyday life, that they draw their impetus from similar sources. This tendency has derived from two central axioms of humanism – the denial of an ontological domain of conditions of action which are relatively independent of situated social activity, and the denial of the relevance and validity of forms of *a priori* theorising. These two, of course, are inextricably linked. The radically empiricist stand of humanist traditions has meant a strict exclusion of rationalist theoretical elements on the grounds that such theorising is ungrounded, a sort of anti-empirical armchair philosophy. Of course, this premise feeds into the parallel ontological one; that there are only the phenomenological forms of the life-world. In other words, social reality is nothing more than people interpreting the meaning of the cultural rules that constitute 'forms of life'.

For the (Chicago school) symbolic interactionist, knowledge of the social world is thus an ongoing practical activity since 'authentic knowledge is not furnished by scientific method but by immediate experience' (Rock 1979, p.183). This has led to a concern with participant observation as an ideal form of research strategy. Participant observation attends to the immediate, given, visible and observable world, and eschews notions of deep structures, systems or orders behind reality, as reified constructs which possess no verifiable reality; immediate experience is the irreducible and only verifiable reality.

As an adjunct to this approach which Bruyn (1966) calls the 'new empiricism' (contrasting it with the traditional empiricism of positivism), *a priori*, analytic knowledge is rejected because as Rock (1979, p.194) says 'such knowledge enforces separations, establishes boundaries and blocks useful access to phenomena'. Direct experience by contrast, 'yields authentic interpretation, and it is produced by attaining some semblance of identity between subject and object'. That is, the participant observer is urged to merge in with the materials of the world he or she is studying. Understanding or knowledge is, thus, an emergent feature (that is, one that is generated and/or freely created by the sociologist) of the actual practice of fieldwork, and the consequent attainment of a union between the observer and his or her subject's world.

The subject's world, in fact, is tapped through a grasping or apprehension of the structures of commonsense meaning that sustain this world. Thus Rock states:

> The structures of everyday meaning are held to represent the *only reality which a sociologist can describe.* They are central in their own right, organizing the selves, processes and institutions which people confront. But they are also properties of nature. Compared with them, *all other kinds of knowledge are ultimately metaphysical and vacuous.* (p.194. My emphasis)

and again,

> The sociologist who looks to immediate understanding will shed 'scientism'. He seeks to explain the common-sense world of his fellows in the language which most nearly approximates its forms. Rather than invoke the alien logic of science he centres his descriptions around common sense. (p.195)

Thus a 'limited paradox', as Rock calls it, is set up, whereby the unsullied experience of the observer, as a member (of the group he is studying) has to be transformed into a sociological account (explanation, description, and so on), *but not into* a scientistic account. That is, the sociological account must approximate, as closely (or as faithfully) to the structures of everyday meaning as possible.

The key research guideline for this strain of symbolic interactionism is inscribed in the transcendental authoritativeness of the empirical world. Blumer (1969, p.33), for instance, castigates the stance in which 'instead of going to the empirical world in the first and last instances, resort is made instead to *a priori* theoretical schemes, to sets of unverified concepts and to canonized protocols of research procedure'. Revealed in this quotation is a highly circumscribed notion of social theory. The only valid 'theory' is that which transmutes descriptions of the everyday worlds of the subjects into a sociological account; an account which must be recognisable as merely a 'gloss' of the original accounts and descriptions, otherwise it will denature these descriptions and undermine their truth.

The phenomenological tradition in sociology exemplified by the ethnomethodological programme, and, more often than not drawing on the work of Schutz (1967), in some respects bears some striking resemblances to the above strain of interactionism. That is, in so far as ethnomethodology concerns itself with an 'experiential empiricism' and a 'personalistic ontology' (Roche 1973) which abandon the reification and objectivism of conventional sociological approaches reflected in positivism and functionalism.

However, there seems to be an even more radical thrust to *some* ethnomethodological positions which assert that society has no objective existence whatsoever and that it exists 'all in the mind' (Roche 1973, p.313). According to this view social structures such as 'class' and 'bureaucracy' exist only in actors' experiences and their linguistic expressions of these experiences. Thus, sociology must concern itself with actors' commonsense understandings and meanings and the linguistically mediated methods they use in achieving successful 'everyday' interaction. In one sense the experiential empiricism and personalistic ontology are fused, giving a characterisation of social reality as nothing other than actors accounts and accounting procedures.

It is clear that both these forms of humanism hold in abeyance any radical distinction between the language and form of social scientific knowledge and the language and form of lay or commonsense knowledge. Although strictly defined there must be some distinction between the social analyst's account and the lay member's

account (otherwise there would be absolutely no need of the sociological account), there should ideally be a minimal discrepancy
between them, otherwise one risks producing a wholly artificial rendering of the social reality under investigation.

In both these versions there is a continual interchange, an assimilation and reabsorption of the languages of social science and
common sense. Schutz's (1967) distinction between first and second
degree constructs expresses this two-way traffic of meaning and language. First-degree constructs refer to the language that lay actors
use 'on the social scene' to use Schutz's phraseology, whilst constructs
of the second order denote the technical meanings and forms of
language that social analysts have erected 'on top' of the first-order
constructs. That is to say, for Schutz, the 'technical' language of
social science is parasitical upon commonsense or everyday language.
As a continuation of this train of thought, Schutz suggests that
the adequacy of concepts or social scientific formulations should be
measured in terms of the degree to which they would be understandable to the actors themselves as a commonsense description of their
own conduct.

It can be seen that there is a loose concurrence between these
humanist positions in so far as they all envisage an extremely fluid
boundary between social analytic descriptions and theorisations and
the linguistic forms of everyday discourse. Ideally, since sociological
description is developed out of actors' accounts, then it must be
capable of retranslation into terms understandable to the actors
themselves. It follows both from this patterning of mutual influences
and the proscription of *a priori* forms of reasoning, that the task of
social analysis cannot be to correct members interpretive knowledge;
rather, the task of social analysis is simply to transpose such knowledge into a more publicly accessible form.

More recently, Giddens has put forward an argument which begins
from a similar premise, that there are close ties and affinities between
sociological and lay language, but then attempts to develop some
finer details which depart from the aforementioned model. Giddens
begins by endorsing Winch's position on this question which he feels
is superior to Schutz's. Winch (1963) suggests that there is a 'logical
tie' between ordinary language and the specialised languages of the
social sciences, but not because (as Schutz suggests), the latter (if
'adequate') are capable of being translated into the former. Giddens
here, is rather scathing of Schutz's formulation in that he feels that
there is no reason to suppose that the adequacy of concepts 'has

anything to do with whether or not such a translation can be affected' (1979, p.247). Rather, the tie exists for Winch 'because the concepts invented by the social scientist presume mastery of concepts applied by social actors themselves in the course of their conduct' Giddens 1979, p.247).

However, Giddens wants to go further than this and suggest that the tie is not simply logical but practical in so far as the social analyst is not simply dependent on the mutual knowledge of those he or she observes. In fact there is a two-way relationship between lay language and the language of social science because 'of the reciprocal "absorption" of social scientific concepts into the social world they are coined to analyse' (Giddens 1987, p.70) which Winch does not consider. Thus, for Giddens there is a circulation in and out of the social world of the concepts invented by social scientists. Giddens states that the 'best and most original ideas in the social sciences, if they have any purchase on the reality it is their business to capture, tend to become appropriated and utilized by social actors themselves' (1987, p.19). Furthermore, says Giddens 'the concepts of the social sciences are not produced about an independently constituted subject-matter, which continues regardless of what these concepts are. The 'findings' of the social sciences very often enter constitutively into the world they determine' (1987, p.20).

Examples of such interchange and reabsorption are fairly thin on the ground in Giddens' work and when they do appear they are of an extremely cursory form. For instance, Giddens suggests, oddly, in my view, that a sociological example of this is the fact that the gathering of social statistics has entered 'in a fundamental way into the constitution of modern societies' because the latter 'could not exist were their demographic characteristics not regularly charted and analysed' (p.21). As Giddens' only sociological example, I find this both puzzling and entirely unconvincing. First, it is not in anything like a clear and unambiguous sense an example of a sociological concept entering into *lay language*. The idea of social statistics and 'statistic gathering' still remains at a fairly high remove from the everyday discourse of most people. This particular example retains a fairly technical connotation and its regular usage is thus limited to a small minority of the educated middle-classes.

Another example that Giddens uses, not this time to indicate the way in which social scientific concepts are absorbed into lay language, but to exemplify the opposite, parasitic relationship of technical concepts on lay concepts, is the one used by Winch from economics;

the notion of 'liquidity preference'. Now even if we were to agree, and I do not, that such a concept is parasitic on lay concepts, in the way both Winch and Giddens suggest, it is nonetheless, a shining example of non-reabsorption into lay language. There could not be a clearer example of non-conformity to the idea of the circulation of social scientific concepts in and out of the social world!

Giddens other main example comes from political theory; 'Modern states could not exist at all were not concepts such as "citizen", "sovereignty", and "government" itself, mastered by those who administer them and those subject to their rule' (p.20). The cursory nature of Giddens' presentation of these examples is evident here. It is certainly an entirely contentious point to suggest that states could not exist without those subject to their rule having mastered concepts like sovereignty! What is meant by 'mastered' here? Is Giddens suggesting that poor people with little or no education have mastered concepts like 'sovereignty'? We might also ask, if this is supposed to be an example of a social scientific concept being absorbed into lay language, whose 'lay language' are we talking about? It is quite feasible to suggest that 'those who administer' modern states will have some 'mastery' of such concepts, but then again we are talking about a minority of the educated middle-class. Giddens' conception of 'lay' concepts or knowledge is peculiarly élitist here. Far from indicating the reciprocal absorption of social scientific concepts these examples suggest a very small degree of absorption from the restricted domains of academic social science itself into the currency of those individuals and groups who have *received* a university education. If such concepts were as easily mastered and absorbed to the extent that Giddens' suggests they are, there would be no reason to offer university courses in (this case in) politics at all!

Giddens compounds this unreality by suggesting that 'Everytime I use a passport to travel abroad I demonstrate my practical grasp of the concept of sovereignty' (p.21). Now, of course, if Giddens was really restricting his discussion solely to himself by the reference to 'I', then how could we disagree! Of course, Tony Giddens is demonstrating his practical grasp of the concept of sovereignty because we know that he is an extremely intelligent man who (presumably), routinely thinks through and connects the abstract connotations of a concept like 'sovereignty' with the very practical activities he happens to be engaged in at the time, in this case using his passport. However, what about the rest of us mere mortals who have difficulty remembering where their passports are, let alone demonstrating our practical grasp of the concept of sovereignty? As applied to the rest of the world, the example is clearly a vast overgeneralisation. Most 'lay' people demonstrate their practical grasp of knowing where their passports are rather than anything as rarefied as the notion of sovereignty. For most people using a passport demonstrates the *practical necessity* of producing an officially stamped document with one's name and photograph on it, before one can enter a foreign country.

As these examples show, Giddens' idea about the reabsorption of social scientific concepts into lay language has some apparent feasibility at the level of mere assertion, but when he attempts to give concrete examples, the whole idea loses credibility. The difficulty that Giddens encounters here is the same one which appears in his idea about the knowledgeability of human agents. Of course, human agents are knowledgeable in a whole number of senses but this does not mean that everybody is equally knowledgeable, nor does it mean that everyone has equal access to the same kinds of knowledge. The difficulty with Giddens' account arises because he rests content simply to assert that all agents are knowledgeable as a counter to those positions in social theory which tend to discount agents reasons, knowledgeability, intentionality, and so on. But this strategy is patently insufficient if the concept of knowledgeability is not unpacked and differentiated, and the notion of the inequality of knowledgeability is not brought in.

It is in these particular respects that despite Giddens' attempt to distinguish his own position from those of Schutz and Winch (and thus, symbolic interactionism and ethnomethodology) there is in fact a high degree of overlap and common ground between Giddens' position and conventional humanism. Although Giddens does see some necessity for the technical languages of social science, an idea which is 'resisted' to varying degrees by both symbolic interactionists and ethnomethodologists, his position is remarkably similar in other respects. First, the idea that there is an unproblematic interchange between lay and social scientific concepts has the effect of 'softening' the boundary between the two. Thus Giddens' position is similar to conventional humanism in that it envisages no qualitative distinctions between lay and social scientific knowledge which would necessitate conceptualising the boundary in 'harder', more distinguishable terms. Second, and related to the former point, the idea that agents are equally knowledgeable (amongst themselves), as well as being knowledgeable in exactly the same senses as social scientific observers (the sharing of mutual knowledge) seems to bring Giddens' position very close to other humanist positions.

The third and most critical sense in which there is an overlap concerns the collapsing of social reality in an ontological model whose boundaries are delineated by the immediate constituting processes of interaction. Giddens' vehement rejection of all forms of objectivism means that the domain and objects of social analysis are exactly the same as in humanist sociologies; that is, the intersubjective world of human agents.

AN ALTERNATIVE VIEW

In what follows I want to suggest an alternative model of the relations between lay and social scientific knowledge which embraces the stratified ontology and epistemology of the social sciences. For the purpose of this model we have to break away from the two central ideas which underlie what I shall for convenience call the 'orthodox' humanist model which I have described above. The first of these key ideas is that there are only two 'languages' that are pertinent to the discussion; that of 'lay' and that of social 'scientific language', the implication being that these two languages are homogeneous unities in their own right. I want to suggest that there are, in fact, two modes of 'technical' language which are employed in social scientific analysis, and that there are also two main modes of lay language that can be the object of social analysis. It follows from this, of course, that the relations between the generic modes of 'lay' and 'scientific language' have to be understood in a far more complex way that is involved in the orthodox model.

Second, it follows in turn from the notion of the increased complexity of relations between lay and social scientific languages that the question of interchange or 'reciprocal absorption' has to be understood in a more subtle way and thus the orthodox model must be considerably amended. Specifically, I want to argue that some technical concepts in social science are not 'parasitic' upon lay language, whilst others are, to a degree, but in a different sense to that assumed by Winch, Giddens and others. Also, I want to suggest that one mode of the (two) technical languages of social science is very rarely (if at all) involved in reciprocal reabsorption into lay languages. Moreover, and as a consequence of this latter, I will argue that there is most definitely a sense in which many technical concepts represent a relatively independent subject matter which continues regardless of what these concepts are. Here, of course, I am challenging Giddens' idea that 'the "findings" of the social sciences *very often* enter constitutively into the world they describe' (my emphasis). On the contrary, whilst *some* findings (and, of course, much depends on what this word means) do enter constitutively into the social world, *many* do not and remain the exclusive province of technical experts.

The elements in this alternative model are represented in Figure 6.1. (page 148) Reading across the figure, the first column denotes which 'author' is making the specific interpretation in question. In this respect we have three possibilities. First we have actors' accounts, in which the focus is on the practical, discursive, interpretive skills of actors 'on the social scene' who employ mutual knowledge (of how to go on) and more general commonsense knowledge in Giddens' terms. Also, such actors may employ any form of discursive 'technical' or specialist knowledge they need in the course of their routine everyday conduct. Second, we have the social analysts' interpretations of the actors' interpretive accounts. That is, the modal form of the 'double hermeneutic' in the orthodox (Giddensian) account. Thirdly, we have the analysts' interpretive accounts couched in terms of either 'structural' or 'technical' meta-languages. I will describe the differences between the two meta-languages presently; what I want to emphasise is that there is a third interpretive level to be considered here, in terms of which the social analyst filters and mediates the other levels of interpretation. This interpretive filtering strictly has two aspects, one of which is more significant.

The first, but less consequential aspect of this filtration process is to do with the fairly diffuse effects of cultural elements like general linguistic structure or background expectancies which act as ordering assumptions in the analyst's interpretation. The second aspect refers to the more systematic background assumptions of a meta-methodological or meta-theoretical nature which guide and order the primary interpretive effects of the other two levels. Networks of concepts that are constitutive of such 'frameworks' as symbolic interactionism, functionalism, 'structuration theory' or 'transcendental realism' house ordering assumptions which produce effects such as determining the status of the other interpretative levels in relation to the cognitive domain of the discourse as a whole.

Moving to the next column we have four main levels of analysis which also identify what I have previously indicated as the four main types of language involved, that is, two types of 'lay' language and two social scientific languages. What I term 'personal' language represents a level of analysis which is usually missing from the orthodox humanist account; the psycho-biographical dimension. This represents individual actors' reasons and accounts, in terms of biographically contextualised experience and commonsense interpretations (see column 3 'interpretive form'). This is a psychological dimension of lay language which is largely ignored in the orthodox view which stresses the linguistic components of cultural 'forms of life'. It is important because it is a source of linguistic resources which are often the subject of social scientific analyses in the form of in-depth and/or biographical interviews.

The feature of the 'interactive' type of lay language which distinguishes it from the above type is that 'mutual knowledge' constitutes its principal content and form. Giddens uses this phrase to connote the Wittgensteinian sense of being able 'to go on' in a 'form of life', that is, to know the tacit rules and the language which are definitive of specific social forms. Irrespective of the tendency to understand such knowledge as tacit in the sense of being difficult to put into words it is clear that such knowledge is routinely rendered into discursive form. As such, mutual knowledge constitutes the frame around which actors reasons, accounts and meanings are arranged. Although Giddens makes a distinction between mutual knowledge and common sense, it is also clear that the two are not mutually exclusive. In the sense in which I am using the term, common sense is very much part of mutual knowledge and vice versa. Common sense simply has a more general reference in relation to routine activity, whilst mutual knowledge refers to 'recipies' for action in situations which demand specific knowledge of how to go on. Quite clearly both mutual knowledge and common sense are interdependent and they constitute a large part of 'the data' upon which the social analyst performs his or her interpretive work.

Below 'interactive' language in column two, is the first of the social scientific or technical languages. I have termed this 'structural' language because it predominately refers to structural features of social life. These are primarily analytic constructs, some of which, whilst not exactly parasitic (that is, 'dependant') upon lay constructs, nonetheless are connected with lay constructs. In these cases there is a sharing of a linguistic component between lay and technical discourses, for example, 'class' or 'bureaucracy' are both lay and technical terms. However, there is only a marginal overlap in the

Interpretive Author	Level of Analysis/ Types of Language	Interpretive Form
Actors' accounts	Personal	Biographically contextualised meanings, accounts, reasons and commonsense interpretations
Analysts' accounts of actors' accounts (Double hermeneutic)	Interactive (forms of life)	Meanings, accounts and reasons in the form of mutual knowledge (how to go on)
Analysts' accounts	Structural	Social organisational features in general in the form of loose conceptual clusterings
(Triple hermeneutic)	Technical	Formally elaborated conceptual networks. Theoretic/analytic pressuppositions

FIGURE 6.1   *The Language of Social Analysis*

meaning senses of these terms. The fact that there is some overlap in a semantic sense and that the terms are common to both lay and technical language has led some ethnomethodologists to suggest that all sociological terms are necessarily 'infected' by commonsense meanings and thus sociological language should face up to its reducibility to commonsense forms. In the context of the overall framework I am presenting here this point of view has to be understood as quite fallacious, based as it is on both an illicit generalisation and a reductionist view of social structure.

To say that concepts like 'class' and 'bureaucracy' are actors' constructs as well as technical concepts of social science is not to presuppose some necessary identity. Such concepts may exist in actors' minds but this does not mean that technical usages of the terms do not have quite different semantic properties. These technical usages may in themselves vary, but they will do so in relation to an environing network of discursive concepts. For example, the technical sense of 'class' will be in part determined by its place in some wider theoretical framework such as functionalist stratification theory or Marxist notions of ownership or non-ownership of the means of production. The lay use of such concepts typically will obey no injunction to assimilate with networks of formally defined concepts, but rather will articulate with, and diffusely enjoin, commonsense ideas and mutual knowledge.

Also, the importance of understanding the objectivist epistemological underpinnings of the technical usages of such terms cannot be overstressed. Although concepts like class and bureaucracy *do* have an 'in-the-minds-of-actors' existential status (as well as an independent 'objective' status), this does not, and cannot arbitrate the objective status of the referents of such concepts. Thus, if someone refuses to believe in the independent existence of the bureaucracy of the electricity board or the taxation office, this will not prevent the independent power of such bureaucracies from putting into motion various legally-backed punitive measures against such an individual. Social structures possess powers that reach beyond the disbelief or warranted doubts of individuals or even groups. In this sense it is an entirely solipsistic manoeuvre to suggest, as some ethnomethodologists have done, that the only access the social analyst has to social structure is through the minds of lay actors (Roche 1973, or that the importance of structural concepts depends upon whether they enter into the minds of lay actors (Benson 1974).

I have suggested that although there are connections between some of the structural concepts of social science and lay language this is not because of a qualitative continuity between these depictions of social reality. Actors' concepts reach into networks of common sense and mutual knowledge for the retrieval of their referential sense, whilst technical concepts reach into formal conceptual networks for theirs. However, apart from the identity of linguistic items used by lay members and social scientists, there are also connections forged by another source.

This involves the sense in which the use of technical constructs presupposes the mastery of other, lower-order concepts. Thus a full understanding of and ability to use the concept of bureaucracy will presuppose mastery of concepts such as 'hierarchy', 'authority', 'specification of duties', and so on. This 'reaching down' into lower-level concepts or linguistic items has to be understood as operating simultaneously with the technical sense of 'reaching up' into formal conceptual networks. Thus, every time a social scientist invokes the technical sense of the term 'bureaucracy' there is a silent but complicated machinery at work which operates in two levels or directions; down into mastered subsidiary concepts and language which are presupposed by the technical invocation, and up into conceptual networks such as Weber's or Marx's theories of bureaucracy.

Now I wish to suggest that, although I have used the same phraseology as Giddens here, the way I understand the 'presupposing of mastery' of lower-order concepts is rather different from Giddens' understanding. Giddens suggests that the use of the technical concepts of social science presupposes mastery of the concepts used by lay actors, and thus he effects and reaffirms the fluid osmotic boundary between lay and technical discourse. But from my point of view it is quite misleading to suggest that all technical concepts involve mastery of lay concepts. This would only apply in my scheme when the analyst is attempting to transpose actors' accounts into sociological interpretation, as in ethnography.

The invocation of technical concepts presupposes mastery of (lower-level) general cultural and symbolic resources made available through language. These latter are no more the exclusive property of lay actors than they are that of social scientists; in principle such communicative resources are available to both. So the connection between lay and social scientific concepts is fashioned by mutually available linguistic referents and not, as in Giddens' scheme, by a parasitic process of mastering and appropriating lay concepts and then transmuting them into technical concepts.

Not all structural concepts are of the type discussed above, where linguistic form is shared by both lay actors and social scientists. Many structural concepts are technical in nature and rarely if ever leak into general lay usage. Concepts such as 'labour market segmentation' or 'modes of organisational compliance' or 'organic' and 'mechanistic' management systems refer to structural features of social life but they have no counterparts in lay discourse and are not parasitic on lay concepts. Of course, as with the other structural concepts, they also presuppose mastery of lower level concepts (in the sense of general linguistic competence).

Typically, such concepts refer to social organisational forms which provide both constraints and facilities in relation to social activity. Usually these concepts have a discursive background in so far as they are associated with clusterings of related concepts which focus upon a similar formal or substantive area of inquiry. For example 'organisational compliance' belongs to a clustering of concepts about organisational control, communication, authority, expertise and so forth. Some of these relatively loose clusterings may also relate to more crystallised or elaborated theoretical networks like dual labour market theory, or theories of the labour process or structuration theory and the like. In so far as they do, then this type of social scientific language shades into the more exclusively 'technical' type.

In Figure 6.1, column two, 'technical' language represents the second of the social scientific languages. As I intimated above, although what I have called 'structural' concepts do shade into the more purely technical types, they are in principle used relatively independently of formally elaborated theoretical networks, and tend to be associated with loose clusterings of concepts similarly focussed on a particular area of inquiry. The technical languages of social science represent what are often referred to as meta-theoretical frameworks, although this term is often used with a certain amount of disdain. Wrongly so, in my opinion, for such embracing frameworks, often couched at a fairly high-level of abstraction, have a very important role to play in the operation of any science, natural or social, regardless of whether or not the importance of this role is actually recognised or acknowledged.

The main distinguishing features of the technical languages of social science concern the level of formal elaboration and interconnection of the constitutive concepts. Such languages have a holistic, organic nature which marks out a domain of questions and answers (problematics) about the nature of social reality as a whole. The concepts within such frameworks have been specifically designed for use within the terms of the framework, thus often their application outside the general terms of the home network is either difficult to accomplish or simply inappropriate. For example, the concept of structure as 'rules and resources recursively implicated in the structuration of social systems', almost by its own definition, is of moment only in the context of the whole conceptual baggage of Giddens' theory of structuration. Similarly, Marx's idea that class relations are determined by ownership/non-ownership of the means of production, maintains its full explanatory force only in the context of the more extended terms of Marx's analysis of capitalism.

The holistic nature of the technical language of social science is connected to another distinguishing feature as compared with the 'structural' language. The holistic nature of these languages requires not only support from allied concepts which represent other contiguous features of social reality, but also support is required from epistemological premises as foundational elements. This is so even if the specific epistemological premises explicitly deny or derogate the importance of epistemological issues – as does Giddens (1984) in his privileging of ontological questions in his exposition of structuration theory.

In order to explicate further the nature of the two modes of scientific language let us go back to the issue of the authors of interpretive claims or procedures. As column one of Figure 6.1 indicates, the first two authorial modes, that is (lay) actors' accounts and social analysts' accounts of these accounts, represent what Giddens has called the 'double hermeneutic' of social scientific analysis. Bhaskar has also noted that 'social reality is pre-interpreted, so that verstehen is a condition of social science' (Bhaskar 1979, p. 204). However, neither of these authors has gone on to distinguish between the social scientists' interpretations of social activity as a technical language, and the kinds of interpretive work involved in what I have termed the structural and technical languages of social science. These latter are involved with interpretive claims not about social activity as such, but about the 'conditions' of such activity. These 'conditions' are to be understood in relation to the different orders of reality that structural and technical languages depict. Thus structural language attempts to represent the social organisational conditions under which social activity takes place, whilst technical language attempts to represent social conditions in a general ontological sense and as delineated by the conceptual network of the discourse.

Taken together as representing the composite conditions of social activity, these two modes of social scientific language essentially contribute a third interpretive standpoint; a 'triple hermeneutic' so to speak. As I have said, the more we approximate towards the purely technical type of language the more we move towards a language which possesses only the most tenuous links (if at all) with lay discourse. The order of interpretation represented by this technical language is engaged in by all social analysts (empirical researchers, social theorists, philosophers) but is very rarely recognised or acknowledged by them. There is always a meta-theoretical assumptive background which does this silent interpretive work even in the case of self-proclaimed agnostics who assert that their work is theory-neutral – for this in itself is a meta-theoretical assumption grounded in a number of supportive presuppositions. This is interpretation of a formal theoretical type which orders the relevance of lower level theoretical strategies or concepts (such as the place of interpretation in social science) and lower level 'data' such as empirical information. Giddens' notion of a 'double hermeneutic' is only pertinent to the situation where an analyst is directly engaged in the interpretive mediation of a particular culture or subculture. But, of course, this does not *exhaust* the role or function of the social analyst, despite Giddens' strong implication to the contrary. This is crystal clear if we examine the work of theorists and philosophers like Giddens and Bhaskar.

Beyond the interpretations of actors' interpretations, their reasons, meanings, accounts and so forth, social theorists are in the business of making theoretical decisions as to the relevance of such things in relation to a much wider theoretical universe of *social objects*. The very notion of a 'double-hermeneutic' itself and its relation to the process of social investigation, the notion of a 'duality of structure' and the 'structuration of social systems as reproduced social relations' are just a few of the theoretically constructed social objects that have a place in Giddens' schema (1976, 1979, 1984). In Bhaskar's work we have the notion of 'transformative activity' the 'transitive' and 'intransitive' objects of scientific knowledge, the 'ontological limits of a social scientific naturalism' 'transcendental realist arguments' and so on. The kind of interpretive assimilation and accommodation that goes on at this formal theoretical level is a very important factor in the adjudication of lower-level theoretical decisions such as the place of interpretation *per se* in social science, the nature of social relations, or the social conditions of intentionality, the nature of social activity and so on.

In the light of the above model of the different types of lay and social scientific languages and the different modes of interpretation involved it is possible to proffer some conclusions on the general relationship between lay and social scientific language. My intention in presenting this model has been to contest the model of the relationship as depicted in the writings of Winch, Giddens and others. I have argued that in general these writers have overstressed the amount of interchange and degree of interdependence between lay and social scientific language. They have seen the relationship in terms of a smooth continuum between a homogeneous lay language on the one hand and a homogeneous specialist language of social science on the other.

This model also stresses that between the two poles of the continuum there is a constant shuffling to and fro of linguistic items. On this view, the language of social science is constantly infused by the lay terms on which it is ultimately based, since the specialist language involves mastery of the concepts that actors use on the social scene. Conversely, the 'concepts and theories invented by social scientists . . . circulate in and out of the social world they are coined to analyse' (Giddens 1987, p. 19), that is, there is a constant reabsorption of social scientific language into lay discourse.

I have questioned the assumptions upon which this model is based, on a number of grounds. The alternative I have presented suggests that both lay and social scientific languages are heterogeneous, and that the relationship between them has to be understood as a disjunctive one rather than a smooth continuum. Phrased slightly differently, the boundary between the two languages is much less permeable than the one indicated in the orthodox model. Thus, the traffic of linguistic items that moves in either direction between these two languages has to be understood as far lighter than has been supposed (especially by Giddens).

Take the case of what I have called technical language. Structuration theory, for instance, is replete with concepts like 'duality of structure', 'double-hermeneutic', 'reproduced social practices', 'time-space distanciation', 'methodological bracketing' and the like, and it would be entirely misleading to say that any of these (or those of any other theoretical framework) derive from (presuppose mastery of) lay language. They presuppose mastery of the English language itself, as well as (at least) preliminary mastery of sociological modes of reasoning (which are in principle accessible to lay members), but quite patently they do not presuppose mastery of genuinely lay forms of discourse, namely the linguistic forms of the groups studied by social researchers. Conversely, it would take an imaginative leap indeed to envisage the terminology of structuration theory being bandied around locales other than the ones inhabited by sociological cognoscenti. To suggest that such language could liberally seep into common circulation seems an overgeneralisation of the first order.

Much the same can be said of what I have terms 'structural' language. Whilst it is true that some 'structural' terms like 'class' and 'bureaucracy' have been appropriated by the social sciences it is not true that such constructs have retained their lay meanings, and thus to suggest that they are somehow (still) based on (or even presuppose mastery of) lay constructs seems something of a romantic illusion. Also, social science employs many structural concepts which are not simultaneously, lay constructs, as the examples of 'labour market segments' or 'organisational compliance' bear out. It is only with regard to social analysts' interpretations of ethnographically researched groups that there *could* be anything like an approximation to the notion of 'regular' interchange between lay and social scientific languages as the orthodox model insists. Although even here on Giddens' own terms he has difficulty providing convincing examples as his discussion of 'sovereignity' and the 'gathering of social statistics' makes eminently clear.

As a coda to this discussion I would like to point out that the alternative model I have set out above bears upon an issue which has been associated with the humanist view whenever this has been proffered; that is, the corrigibility or otherwise of (lay) actors' accounts. The thoroughbred humanist writers in the symbolic interactionist and phenomenological traditions have tended towards the view that actors' beliefs and accounts are incorrigible and that it is the social analysts' task to render these beliefs and accounts as faithfully as possible. However, writers like Giddens and Bhaskar have inclined towards a view which suggests that whilst it is not necessarily a primary concern of social science to 'correct' the false beliefs or accounts of lay actors, nonetheless, in principle, such accounts are corrigible. Now what I have said about the relationship between lay and social scientific language in general would seem to endorse this specific claim, but it would also set it in a much broader context than the one licensed by the humanist model. Indeed, it may be the case that some aspects of actors' accounts are corrigible in the face of the findings of social science, and it may also be the case that there are elements of actors' accounts that remain 'uncorrectable' (as Giddens suggests is the case with mutual knowledge). However, it must also be remembered that much of the language of social science is not an attempt to represent actors' interpretations of their social activity, or an attempt to represent the forms of activity; rather, it is an attempt to conceptually model the elements constitutive of the conditions of social activity.

At this juncture I would like to steer the discussion back to an issue which I addressed more fully in chapters 2, 3 and 5; the epistemological debate between empiricism and rationalism. In this case I want to connect this issue both to the previous discussion of the relation between lay and social scientific language, and also to the question of conceptual discovery in social research. In those earlier chapters I suggested that realism must confront the empiricist-rationalist debate head-on, and not misguidedly assume that the problem of empiricism has been transcended. Specifically, I have suggested that the dominant empiricist orthodoxy must be leavened by an incorporation of rationalist principles, particularly in relation to the importance of conceptual networks in the knowledge process.

At the same time, however, my argument has been that empiricism cannot be rejected totally for it possesses at least *some* purchase on the understanding of social reality. The crucial mistake of empiricists and positivists alike has been to conceive of empiricism as the only valid epistemological position in social science. Realists (particularly Harré) have unwittingly buttressed this view by refusing to engage with objectivist or macro positions in social science which depend on rationalist forms of argument. On the other hand, rationalists such as Althusser and Poulantzas have embraced objectivist and rationalist positions to the dogmatic exclusion of interactionist and phenomenological positions. I suggested in chapter 3 that a useful realist position would be one which evaluated forms of knowledge in terms of the extent to which they circumvented the extremes of both empiricist and rationalist positions, and thus avoided the arbitrary restrictions on knowledge that flow from these positions.

CONCEPTUAL INNOVATION IN QUALITATIVE RESEARCH

I want now to apply these prescriptions to a specific aspect of the problem of conceptual innovation in field research. At certain junctures I will draw upon the previous discussion of lay and social scientific concepts in support of some of the points I wish to advance. The specific notion of fieldwork on which I wish to focus derives from the humanistic variant of the symbolic interactionist tradition in sociology which, as I have described previously, accentuates the importance of actors' experiences, perceptions and attitudes in the quest for authentic knowledge. One strand in this humanistic tradition is the 'grounded theory' approach of Glaser and Strauss (1967).

Much of the distinctiveness of this approach stems from an explicit rejection of the scientistic or objective empiricism of positivism and an endorsement of an experiential or phenomenological empiricism. Thus, the authors reject the primacy accorded to quantitative data based on the fixed-choice questionnaire survey in the positivist vision of social science and, instead, emphasise the importance of qualitative data, in-depth and semi-structured interviews as well as the range of participant and non-participant observational techniques. An attractive feature of grounded theory is that it directs primary attention to the problem of theoretical discovery or conceptual innovation. In this sense it moves away from the typical positivist tendency towards the verification (or falsification) of existing theories and theoretical frameworks via the employment of the hypothetico-deductive method. Instead, grounded theory attends to the possibilities of exploratory fieldwork and theory-generation.

Now this emphasis on the idea of grounded theory and fieldwork as vehicles for theoretical discovery seems entirely laudable and should occupy a central place in any realist scheme. This is for several reasons. First, an emphasis on conceptual innovation as an *outcome* of empirical research acts as an insurance against the theoretical stagnation that attends the verificationist or falsificationist mode of empirical research under the aegis of positivism. It also acts against the stultification of theory that derives from dogmatic and exclusive commitments to particular theoretical frameworks such as functionalism, Marxism, ethnomethodology and so on. The inability to stray beyond the conceptual confines of one's favoured home theory may or may not be coupled with the extreme rationalist tendency to deny the importance of external object referents to theoretical discourses, as in Althusserian Marxism.

Secondly, an emphasis on conceptual discovery or innovation may open up fruitful lines of dialogue between theoretical and substantive problems concerning the macro-micro interface of social reality, or what is otherwise termed the agency-structure problem in sociology. In this respect such an emphasis can identify potential areas of analytic fusion or synthesis between the experiential, interactive aspects of social reality and the structural and organisational conditions of social activity. However, a serious caveat must be entered here concerning the ability of grounded theory to generate such fusions or syntheses of macro and micro features.

This, of course, concerns the problem of the empiricist epistemological basis of the humanist tradition. A realist position would need to go beyond the entrapment in knowledge of the experiential, phenomenological world of social activity and attempt to incorporate the structural and technical conditions of the activity. So, to achieve a viable realist position the terms in which the grounded theorists have couched the idea of discovery through research must be extended. This extension includes the proviso that what I have called the structural and technical discourses of social science must be included as a locus of relevance *vis-à-vis* the development and discovery of knowledge. That is, *a priori* forms of knowledge produced through the (more or less integrated) clustering and interlocking of concepts must be integrally involved with theoretical discovery via qualitative research under certain conditions.

One important condition involves identifying and perceiving the technical discourses of social science as theoretically *open* conceptual universes. This can be achieved in two main ways. Firstly, and of course subject to rigorous epistemological templates, this can be achieved by reidentifying extant 'closed' theoretical discourses as potentially open conceptual universes, either at the level of whole frameworks, for example, symbolic interactionism, functionalism, Marxism, or at the level of specific authors, such as Parson's systems theory. Secondly, and perhaps more importantly, it can be achieved by producing new conceptual frameworks by filtering through and fusing with the structural concepts which cluster around similar substantive problems and areas and which may or may not be continuous with the more integrated clusterings present in the technical discourses. Of course, instances of 'fusion' have to be produced against a background of epistemological criteria of comparability.

In this manner, the notion of discovery can be reformulated to include both the idea of substantive embeddedness (this term involves an important differentiation with the idea of 'grounding') of concepts, and the idea of the relatively autonomous properties of knowledge produced through conceptual interlocks. This approach leaves the interactionist's original formulation of discovery through grounded theory intact, whilst also indicating a radical departure from it. Briefly, the implication of this is that the grounded theorists notion of discovery, although valid for *certain* purposes and questions, is nonetheless a limited form of discovery which is itself based on an inherently limited form of knowledge, namely, empiricism. Thus, whilst the formulation of theoretical discovery that I am arguing for here does not vitiate the grounded theorists own formulation in the sense of rendering it baseless (indeed, I shall argue later that it is indispensible for certain types of problem), it does underline its inherent limitations by providing a non-empiricist alternative.

The formulation that I am proposing here endorses the idea of the potential substantive embeddedness of concepts and theory relating to social interaction or forms of life, thus necessitating discovery through first-hand field research. This is quite different from the interactionist idea of the inherent 'groundedness' of *all* genuine theory. The idea of embeddedness involves the possibility of using first-hand field research methods in conjunction with rational and discursive modes of theoretical knowledge. I shall be illustrating this in more detail presently, but the areas which spring immediately to mind, to which these ideas can be of relevance, are the related ones of class, occupation and labour markets. In these areas the gap between the grounded theories of the interactionists and the so called *a priori* theories of objectivist social analysts is at its widest. Thus, class analysts such as Wright (1979), Poulantzas (1973) and Althusser (1969) concern themselves with the objective features of the class structure, relations of power and domination, conjunctions between classes and occupational groupings, and so forth, and eschew, or even reject, interactionist analyses and/or analyses of interaction. At the other end of the spectrum, interactionists concern themselves with occupational socialisation, commitment (subjective) careers, self-images and the like, and reject or lose sight of objective relations of power and domination. (Forgetting for the moment the ideological and political reasons for such mutual rejections.)

The idea of theoretical discovery and embeddedness that I am developing here attempts to build one kind of bridge between such studies by connecting the study of objective constraints (relations of power and domination) with the study of inter-subjective experience, careers, interaction, and so on. This particular bridge requires the adoption of a post-empiricist position on the nature of knowledge and theory. Thus, the idea of the embeddedness of theory and concepts is derived from a position which suggests that knowledge (of interaction, behaviour, and so forth) is not exclusively *given* by and in the apprehension of empirical reality by the researcher. Rather it suggests that in large part knowledge and theory can be profitably conceived as the outcome of a dialectical interplay between relatively autonomous and prior theoretical knowledge about the objective features of social life (particularly structures of power and domination), *and* the revelatory activities of field research.

By 'revelatory activities of field research' I mean the ability of the researcher to generate concepts and theory *in situ*, through confrontation with data, empirical reality. However, the meanings of these concepts are not given to them exclusively by and in their concurrence with the commonsense reality of the people (interactants) who are being studied. I develop examples of these later but briefly, I am thinking of such theoretical concepts as 'segmental labour market' which relates to the career experience of (dramatic) actors, for example; or the concept of 'typification' which attempts to depict a form of career control over actors by casting personnel. (For more detail see below.)

Similarly, the 'generation' element indicates that such theory and concepts are not simply determined by some pre-conceived (objectivist) theoretical scheme; thus theory and concepts are genuinely revealed (uncovered) by research, but their 'meanings' or referents are significantly (although not completely) conditioned by 'structural' or 'technical' discourse about objective factors. The interplay element between revelation and pre-giveness in the generation of theory will be illustrated in more detail later.

However, to continue with the example alluded to before, the study of the commonsense reality and occupational experience of some group, for example, actors, jazz musicians, taxi drivers, can be linked to such factors as prior structures of power in occupational labour markets through the idea of substantive embeddedness by conceiving of the experience of practitioners and significant others (that is, that which is to be uncovered by research), as in part a function of these relatively autonomous objective structures. (It must be noted here that this formulation has nothing in common with those that insist that behaviour, experience and so on, *are* completely determined by such structures.) This formulation attempts to theorise the links between objective constraints and subjective experience, or, in other words, to theorise the links between macro and micro levels of sociological analysis.

However, as I have pointed out in previous chapters, my position does not require a total (and rather arrogant) dismissal of empiricist knowledge in the manner of some authors (D. and J. Willer 1973; Althusser 1969; Hindess 1977); it merely registers the arbitrary limitations upon theoretical knowledge that empiricism enforces. Thus, if knowledge is exclusively lodged in the given, phenomenal, experienced world, then our knowledge is limited to our sensory perceptions of that world. In relation to my own version of realism the kind of rational/theoretical knowledge to which I allude refers to knowledge of 'real' mechanisms or structures which underlie the phenomenal forms of experience social reality (participant observation, fieldwork and so on).

One of the main mechanisms in this respect is what I have termed elsewhere the contextual conditions of interaction (Layder 1981). Thus, on this view, the objects of study (or knowledge) are *not only* groups of 'people doing things together' (Becker 1970), 'behaviour and interaction' (Glaser and Strauss 1967) or 'social activity' (Giddens 1984) but also the contextual conditions which provide parameters to these phenomena and which facilitate their emergence in the first place. According to this argument the phenomena themselves, for example, interaction, behaviour, and so on, do not provide *all* their own conditions of existence, although they do provide some. For example, what happens in one episode of interaction will to some extent influence the actions and behaviour of the same people in a subsequent episode, as will the capacities of those people to be purposive (intentional) and self-reflexive in their behaviour. However, these events and capacities are not the only generative conditions that need to be considered; the social contextual environment of the interaction (bureaucratic organisation, type of labour market) will also constrain and facilitate various forms of behaviour and interaction.

Grounded theory only attends (and then only implicitly) to the conditions of existence that are produced by the phenomena themselves; the cumulative, productive and creative nature of social activity itself. Thus, the critique of empiricism alerts us to an important consequence of the grounded theorist's position; it tends to reduce social reality to its phenomenal forms, and thus social *structure* becomes nothing other than various kinds of interactional manifestation. This is basically because of a fear of 'reifying' social reality by the use of such objective terms as structure, system and so on, as referring to supra-individual, relatively impersonal properties of social reality.

Now, whilst their are some reified usages of the concept of structure such that structures as it were, exist *totally* independently of human agency (Berger and Luckman 1967, p. 106), this reified form of usage must not be confused with the idea that objective (for instance, contextual) structures have a *relative independence*. That is, although they depend upon *human beings* in the general sense of that term, to operate them, they do not depend upon specific individuals or specific social groups (in the sense that the capitalist economic system is not dependent on say, prostitutes, for its continued existence). Also, although historically, objective structures may have been brought into existence by the actions of certain groups and individuals, it is also true that once in existence and institutionalised, over time such structures although themselves in process, attain a pre-established, though not 'alien' facticity to the people subject to them, and in fact constrain and facilitate their actions and behaviour. (See chapter 5.)

Unless these distinctions between reified and non-reified usages of the term structure are made, then the anti-reification lobby merely courts a form of empiricist reductionism whereby objective, pre-established social structures of power and domination are explained by reference to the productive activities of people in routine encounters. In this sense grounded theory merely describes interactive realities without inquiring into or theorising the wider external, contextual conditions of these interactive realities.

SOCIAL ACTIVITY AND EXPLANATORY CONCEPTS

In relation to the arguments developed above, I want to further argue that the grounded theorists' view of what counts as an explanation or an account of social behaviour is only partial. This is exemplified in Rock's view that 'the structures of everyday meaning are held to represent the only reality which a sociologist can describe' and 'the sociologist . . . seeks to explain the commonsense world of his fellows in the language which most nearly approximates its forms (1979, p. 94–5). Glaser and Strauss's view is a little less strong, although their criteria of the validity of a theory, that it should 'fit' empirical reality and be 'relevant' to those people who are the objects of the study, makes most sense in relation to those ideas. Thus, the criteria of an adequate account revolve around the sociologist's ability to grasp the commonsense reality, and thus the language, of the people studied.

It should also be noted here that for all their differences, and purported differences in derivation and emphasis from the interactionists just cited, and between themselves, both Winch (1963) and Giddens (1976 and 1979) have construed the main problem of accounting for activity as one of interpretation – for Winch the intelligibility of rule-governed action, and for Giddens the penetration of frames of meaning. That is to say, I am here noting a parallel anti-positivist concern with apprehending the meaningful and intentional nature of conduct, a concern which indeed is shared by most existential and humanist forms of sociology (Schutz 1967; Douglas 1977; Garfinkel 1967). At that point, however, the similarity ends, in so far as the interactionists are less concerned with the philosophical analytic problems of 'interpretation' and more concerned with getting into the field and actually doing research. However, in all these humanist (anti-positivist) strands of thought there is a concurrence over the idea that the objects to be studied and explained are social behaviour, conduct, interaction and so forth, and that this is basically an interpretive task. As I pointed out in the earlier part of this chapter, there is also a rather more loose concurrence over the idea that there is, or should be, some connection between the language and meanings that social scientists use to describe or explain social behaviour, and the language and meanings of the actors which they attempt to depict on the social scene', to use Schutz's phrase.

I want to argue that to explain or account for social activity we must recognise that the social relations that provide the contextual conditions of interaction exert a structuring effect on it, and must be brought into the analysis to provide a fuller account. Following from this, and the arguments of the previous chapter, in some instances the language and meanings that sociologists use to account for social activity have no necessary connection with lay language and concepts (that is, the actor's commonsense world). Neither of these two statements is to be confused with ideas such as 'actors' reasons for their behaviour are to be discounted', or, that the model of human behaviour lying behind such arguments is a mechanistic or rigidly determinist one (Giddens), or that social actors are treated like cultural dopes (Garfinkel), or in any sense that lay actors are derogated (Giddens 1979). Indeed the model of social activity that lies behind this version of realism is that it is intentional, meaningful, creative and evinces the 'knowledgeability' of the actors concerned.

However, my argument also implies that such attributes of behaviour occur within delimited social contexts, and that therefore the relationship between these attributes (for instance, intentionality) and the contextual circumstances under which they are actualised, must be explored. In this respect the idea that actors are all, as it were, equally knowledgeable about the conditions of their social existence can be taken to the opposite extreme (for instance, Giddens), to that which accords knowledgeability no importance at all, as in certain forms of structural determinism. The idea that social actors, particularly in the practical (but also discursive) sense, 'know what they are doing' so to speak, and that this should be taken into consideration when accounting for their behaviour, should not be confused with the idea that all sociological explanation must begin and end with an analysis of actors' reasons for their conduct. My argument here is concerned to underline the fact that in many cases it is profitable to conceive of actors' accounts of their actions as only becoming sociologically meaningful in terms of the simultaneous analysis of objective conditions of enactment.

This is the upshot of the realist position I am outlining, but as I said before, this does not vitiate empiricist knowledge in its own right. Empiricism like any other mode of knowledge, has its own internal criteria of validity. My position here is that the usefulness of knowledge derived by empiricist means depends upon answers to the following questions:

(1) What needs to be known? That is, what does the researcher want to find out?

(2) (a) How are the objects of the analysis/research (for instance, data), to be understood? That is, what epistemological basis determines the form of the knowledge? Which leads to:

(b) What *range* or *scope* of explanation is required? For example, do we simply want an explanation in terms of the situational mechanics of social activity or do we also require knowledge of its contextual conditions?

It is in terms of questions of this sort that my position would allow, and indeed require, that in *certain senses* the micro-world of interaction has to be understood in terms of first-hand experience. Thus, if the researcher wants to know what is 'going on' in an episode of social interaction, in the sense of trying to understand the intentions (plans, objectives) of the interactants, then first-hand experience and involvement on the social scene is invaluable. For example, in terms of Glaser and Strauss's own work on the awareness contexts surrounding dying patients, or in terms of Laing and Esterson's (1964) study of schizophrenic women, some first-hand knowledge of the internal mechanics of situated interactions is a necessary prerequisite to theorising about such problems.

Thus also, concepts such as 'closed awareness contexts' or 'repressions of autonomy' attempt to evoke the interactional and experiential realities of the participants involved. These concepts are attempts to forge an isomorphic correspondence between an observer's description or evocation of what is going on at a conceptual level, with what is actually going on. In this context, criteria such as 'relevance' (to those involved) and 'fit' with reality , become meaningful criteria. The need to answer such questions as what is actually 'going on', that is, what is being done by the participants in this episode of interaction, requires phenomenological, and thus, empiricist knowledge.

However, if one requires a wider understanding of a particular episode of interaction, which includes knowledge of the contextual conditions under which it occurs, phenomenological knowledge in itself is not enough. Thus, if one wants to know how the career experiences and behaviour of (dramatic) actors relates to the labour market for actors and the occupational organisation of acting, it does not suffice to rely on actors' reasons for their behaviour or attitudes to, or accounts of, their career experiences. One needs objective knowledge of the nature of the labour market itself and its segmental structure, and how these create the parameters for career experiences. Thus, theoretical concepts which relate and are 'relevant' to actors and their subjective career experiences, such as the segmental labour market and the structure of occupational control and domination which maintains it, are not attempts to produce isomorphic correspondences between the concepts themselves and the behaviour and experience to which they relate, and which they partly explain. In this respect the notion of 'fit' here is irrelevant. Similarly, the notion of 'relevance' in the sense of concepts being recognisably understandable to participants as descriptions of 'what is going on' in their routine occupational encounters is a misapplication of the term. In this sense, such concepts as 'segmental labour market' and so on, may play no part in the day-to-day lives or commonsense realities of participants. However, in a quite different sense these concepts are 'relevant' to such participants because they express a parallel, but not necessarily observable reality which underpins and to a significant extent 'produces' their experienced worlds. Such concepts do not derive simply from qualitative research of an occupational group; in fact they derive mainly from theories of the labour market, and structures of occupational power and control; but they do express the social contextual reality that encompasses the lived experiences of participants.

What goes for purely structural or technical concepts also goes for concepts which are more closely related to actual modes of behaviour. A case in point is a concept I developed in relation to the analysis of the career in acting. The concept of *typification* relates to the way in which status mobility in the career is mediated to a large extent by significant others in the occupation who control the casting of shows, programmes and so on, and thus control access to jobs. In this sense 'typification' refers to a rationalised, behavioural and attitudinal solution to an occupational problem routinely encountered by casting directors, namely, how to 'cast' a production. In this light, the typification of actors by casting directors can be more clearly understood by contrasting it with the idea of 'type-casting', whereby some actors or actresses are constantly cast in one type of role. Type-casting, of course, can lead to career immobility, whereas 'typification' normally has the opposite effect: the facilitation of upward career mobility. This is because typification refers to the process whereby an actor or actress becomes typified by casting personnel as being relevant to a certain *range of theatrical roles*. Being 'thought of' in this way by those who control career progress, facilitates employment opportunities in an occupation in which unemployment is the norm. Also, typification is an element or aspect of the actions and behaviour of casting personnel which tends to reproduce and reaffirm the extant power and status hierarchy within the occupation as a whole, including the non-acting sectors.

Now whilst the concept of typification was generated *in situ* so to speak, as a result of first-hand field research, it is not a term which casting directors would use. In this sense it is not a description or conceptual representation of casting directors' reasons or accounts of their own behaviour. Moreover, whilst it does tell us something about the social activity and orientations of casting personnel, it is not couched in a language which endeavours to approximate (the forms of) the commonsense worlds of actors or casting directors. However, the concept of typification is an attempt to represent the behaviour of casting directors as partly conditioned by the occupational environment in which they work. In this sense the behaviour of casting directors (and others) is seen in relation to its function in the *mediation of control* over actors' careers, and thus, of access to various segments of the labour market.

In this respect it is misleading to conceptualise the human being simply as the original and spontaneous, single most important locus of action (Harré 1979). Human beings are required to act in terms of the constraints of the social environment, but not simply in a behaviouristic or mechanistic stimulus-response way. To posit some degree of 'acquiescence' as it were, to constraints (and facilities) of social contexts is not to posit a cultural dope who cannot reflect upon and formulate his or her actions, or intentionally and purposively 'do otherwise', for example, reject constraints. It merely points to the fact that there are minimal (but also, differential) levels of conformity to socially organised activities (for instance, work tasks) which are required in order to 'stay in' the activity itself, or in order for it to be legitimately claimed that somebody is *still engaged* in a certain line of activity.

Take the example of the casting director; at the simplest level he or she must conform to the demands of casting itself. They must appraise actors for future roles by seeing shows, meeting actors formally and informally, and thus building a stock of knowledge for future use. However, there are other constraints which, whilst not absolutely minimal in this sense, nonetheless cannot be flouted without due consideration of the consequences. The most important in this respect is the 'star system' whereby established or 'name' actors and actresses are hired to perform the main roles in a play or a film, so that its potential success (marketability) will be at least partly ensured. The commercial constraints under which casting directors usually operate, necessitate a certain due deference to the star system regardless of whether they offer this as a reason for their behaviour or not.

Finally, I would like to make a few comments on an idea which I have already alluded to, and which is intimately connected to what I will call this undue preoccupation with reasons and accounts, and that is the question of the purported knowledgeability of (social) actors of the conditions under which they operate. Of course, social actors are knowledgeable about the conditions under which they act in the sense that they know what they are doing and are self-reflexive about the kind of workaday world in which they live out their lives; indeed, if they did not, or were not, then they would indeed be *real* morons or dopes as opposed to merely cultural ones. Also, it does not require much 'empirical observation' to proffer the idea that given half a chance most people would be able to theorise about such knowledge in terms of their own conceptions or commonsense theorisations about the world, or the particular sector of the world in which they live. However, to say this is not the same thing as saying that social actors (without saying anything about their capabilities or potentialities) know about the objective social conditions and factors that contextualise their behavioural world.

To adopt a position which accedes just this, that people do not *necessarily* have knowledge of such conditions (indeed why should they) is not, nor does it lead to, a derogation of the lay actor. Only an imputation of the *impossibility* of people acquiring such knowledge through lack of ability and the like, would lead to such a derogation. More positively, the adoption of such a position does square up to the reality that certain kinds of structural or technical social scientific concepts may remain more or less the exclusive province of those responsible for producing them in the first place. To insist that there is always some necessary connection between lay concepts and those of sociologists (an issue which subsumes others, such as whether or not common sense is corrigible) is an overgeneralisation which fails to register the existence of a body of technical sociological concepts which have no direct connection with the commonsense worlds of members but which nonetheless attempts to account for this world.

LANGUAGE AND SOCIAL RESEARCH REVISITED

The above discussion has indicated an interesting complication *vis-à-vis* the earlier discussion of the relation between lay and social scientific language. It has pointed to the possibility of the existence of a special type of structural concept which distinguishes it from the kinds of structural concepts that were the subject of the earlier discussion. There are two principal distinguishing features involved. First, such concepts are genuinely synthetic in a way which other structural concepts are not. That is, they bridge the gap between the social organisational conditions of activity and the experiential, attitudinal and behavioural dimensions of such activity. These concepts do attempt to represent some aspect of the phenomenal world of social agents, but at the same time they represent it as partly conditioned by its social context. However, these concepts remain genuinely part of the stock of social scientific language in so far as they retain technical meanings which are not reducible to, or parasitical upon linguistically mediated forms of life. In this sense they exhibit the same properties that I outlined earlier for structural concepts which are not shared by lay actors.

The second distinguishing feature of these concepts is that they are, to a large extent, embedded in substantive data such that they can be only fully revealed by a conjunction of theoretical filtration and qualitative field research. Such direct confrontation with the phenomenal world can help tease out the behavioural implications of structural concepts. However, being structural concepts in the first place means that their full implications are never simply given by the revelatory activities of research. A dialectical interplay with a process of theoretical filtration based on the connections between cognate concepts is necessary to produce the explanatory power of such intermediary or bridging concepts. In the case of the concept of 'typification', theories and concepts of control and power in a segmented labour market were required to inform its 'mediation of control' function.

Throughout this discussion as a whole I have endeavoured to set out a schema which expands the explanatory basis of realism with regard to the question of the relation of lay and social scientific language and the question of conceptual innovation and qualitative research. Both of these feed into the larger question of the relation between theory and evidence in social science. My intention has been to open up areas of debate and discussion around this general issue by questioning some of the current orthodoxies in social science with which realists have either directly concurred or, which, through lack of protest, they have silently endorsed. I have also tried to push back the boundaries of accepted practice both on the question of the generation of concepts through research and on the broader question of the nature of social scientific knowledge.

My strategy has been what I would describe as one of 'disciplined expansion', with the emphasis on the 'disciplined'. Thus, whilst recognising the quite formidable problems that attend any dogmatic and exclusive adherence to either empiricism or rationalism, I have adopted a position which tries to rescue the necessary component of cognitive adequacy (or truth) in both of them. I have attempted to trace out the implications of this presupposition for a more encompassing realist position on the theory-evidence relation as it is reflected in the concepts and language of social research and everyday life.

7 The Prospects for Realism

Throughout this book I have tried to identify a cluster of important issues and problems that tie in with the project of realism as it relates to sociology and social psychology in particular, and to the social sciences more generally. This has involved identifying the key tenets of the realist project and subjecting them to a constructive critique. The 'constructive' element is all important since my intention has been to lend support to realism while endeavouring to come to terms with what I take to be its shortcomings as it is presently constituted. Of necessity, this has required a serious engagement with formal issues of a philosophical and theoretical nature, although throughout, I think I have managed to retain sight of more down-to-earth matters.

It is the resolution of this paradox between formal philosophical concerns and concrete empirical issues of research and social analysis that presents, perhaps, the most formidable challenge to a realism which aspires to anything more than a peripheral relationship with mainstream practitioners of social science. One of the central messages of this book has been to suggest that the 'resolution' of this paradox cannot be conceived of in a conventional way, as an eventual dissolution of either the formal or the concrete sides of the equation.

Undeniably, an obstacle to the widespread assimilation of realist concerns is, and will continue to be, the studious indifference of many social analysts and researchers who demand to know what difference a concern with such seemingly abstruse philosophical matters will make to their thinking and practice. This indifference perhaps will be conjoined with either a muted or an open hostility to philosophy and philosophical concerns in general. For those who worry about the demon of philosophy the cry is 'let us emancipate ourselves from the grip of this monster and allow sociology and social psychology to affirm their autonomy as empirical sciences'. Now, as a corrective to this paranoiac reaction, my argument has not been, nor will it ever be, that philosophy and philosophising are to be revered for their own sakes. There will continue to be irrelevant, pedantic and arrogant philosophical sophistry as there has always been, just as the social sciences have had their fair share of trivial and myopic (mainly empirical) pursuits. What I have tried to do is

170

point out that there are some ineradicable philosophical problems, independent of particular philosophical systems or modes of philosophising, but which are endemic to the practice of social science.

In my view the upshot of this is that sociologists and social psychologists must acknowledge the analytic space that only certain forms of philosophical argument may fill, and then open the door to interdisciplinary dialogue in this respect. Thus, for example, the claim that sociology should shake off the 'yoke of philosophy' and become an independent science only makes sense if the questions of what a 'science' is, and what it is capable of, are not taken for granted. Thus, the question of the form and nature of social science has to be subjected to the kind of philosophical analysis that I have undertaken in this book. In this sense the resolution of the paradox between formal philosophical issues and concrete empirical research cannot be resolved simply and solely in favour of the latter. The very nature of empirical research will be influenced by issues concerning the underlying vision of social science upon which it is based, and the specific methodological prescriptions that it entails.

What I am arguing for here is reminiscent of some of the arguments made by the humanistic philosophers Winch (1958), and Louch (1969), although in other respects my arguments run counter to theirs. The point of similarity lies in Winch's call for philosophy to rid itself of its 'underlabourer' role *vis-à-vis* social analysis. In this respect philosophy has a considerably more important part to play than the simple clearing away of linguistic confusions prior to the 'real business' of empirical research. The arguments in this book endorse the view that philosophy has a more profound and substantial role to play in social analysis. In this sense philosophy and social research must be equal partners in social analysis.

It is this insistence on an equal footing that sets apart my own ideas from those of Winch, for he wishes to arrogate social analysis *in toto* for philosophy. In my view, this is not only a hopelessly arrogant aim, but also a hopelessly impossible one. There is, in this respect, greater merit in Louch's view that there is an irreducibly empirical dimension to social analysis. However, as I argued in chapter 5, Louch's attempt to conceive of all social analysis as a species of moral explanation fails to apprehend the variegated nature of social reality, and partly as a result tends to resort to a variant of Winch's philosophical imperialism, although admittedly, less extreme.

What Winch and Louch fail to see is that while *verstehen* (including here, hermeneutics and phenomenology) is an undeniably important aspect of social analysis, it does not exhaust the possibilities. In this sense, the humanistic project which Winch and Louch represent in philosophy is but one version of social analysis or social 'science'. 'Science' here is understood as a disciplined system of cognition designed to represent a specific subject matter; in this case forms of social life. In this sense the humanistic project can be understood as a distinct vision of social science, and thus a specific characterisation of this 'science'. It is not, as Winch and Louch imply *a*scientific. It is, rather, against versions of science such as positivism and realism which retain elements of the natural science paradigm. Of course, and as I hope I have made plain, when viewed in the context of the whole array of social scientific discourses, it is not as clear-cut as this, since several versions of realism in social science draw very heavily on what are primarily humanistic strands of social theory, such as symbolic interactionism and ethnomethodology.

Not only do Winch and Louch fail to see the partiality of their claims about the nature of social analysis (and the built-in assumptions about a 'science' of the social that attend such claims), but also they espouse an unnecessarily restricted notion of the range and type of objects that should, or can come under the scrutiny of social analysis. In common with the empirically-minded social scientific humanists they restrict the ontological depth of the social to the phenomenological forms of the life world. This, it must be emphatically noted, is not simply a formalistic issue of little import to social research. It is a restriction (and an artificially imposed one at that) which strikes at the very heart of substantive analysis; thus, the restriction of ontological depth is also a restriction on empirical depth. It is a foreclosure on the possible range of empirical questions and types of empirical objects that can be described or explained within the conventional terms of social analysis.

There can be no clearer demonstration of the way in which philosophical or theoretical presuppositions about the nature of social scientific analysis profoundly shape the very findings that result from social research. In this particular case the shaping is of a negative nature in so far as it is an unnecessary constriction of the explanatory power and scope of analysis. Much the same can be said of those empirical sociological purists who insist that sociology is or should be autonomous with regard to philosophical issues. Such a stance is in itself based upon the presuppositions of theory-neutrality and a naive correspondence theory of knowledge, both of which have been rightly criticised for their cognitive inadequacy.

Understanding the partiality and limited applicability of claims to truth implicit in the positivist and humanist versions of social science is an important component of the philosophical task posed by the very existence of social science. Of course, realism itself is just as much an integral part of this. What realism has done is to destroy the myth that positivism was the only true exemplar of the natural and social sciences. One of the themes of this book has been that a central weakness of the realist project in this regard has been its inability to sift through the divergent truth claims and to arrange them in an order which makes sense of the realist project itself.

Essentially it was to this task that I addressed myself in chapter 2, and this theme has subsequently informed the rest of the book. My premise was that not only has realism thus far failed to situate itself in relation to the markedly stratified nature of social scientific discourses (including a concern with their variable forms and functions), but also, it has not taken seriously enough the implications of the debate between rationalism and empiricism. This lack is clearly evident in the work of the prominent writers on realism, who, while solidly opposed to the dominance of positivist empiricism, have given little attention to the possibilities of forms of rationalist knowledge and their relation to empiricism. Writers such as Harré and Bhaskar have skirted the full implications of this because of the implied transcendence of the empiricist-rationalist debate. Stated bluntly, the implication has been that the methodological prescriptions of realism, *ipso facto*, have outmoded empiricist social science, but quite where this leaves empiricist modes of knowledge and what role rationalist influences may have, have not been explored.

These authors also seem to employ a unitary notion of empiricism which stands in the way of an appreciation of the more subtle epistemological ramifications of the issue. My position has been to suggest that while a social science based entirely on empiricist foundations will inevitably be impoverished, the whole empiricist tradition cannot be written-off entirely. I have suggested that certain elements of empiricism are necessary to a full understanding of social life, but that the inherent limitations of an exclusively empiricist outlook must be acknowledged. As a counterbalance to the recognition of the limited but essential cognitive force of empiricism, my argument has emphasised the pressing need to incorporate rationalist forms of knowledge and draw them into the fold of the current, predominately empiricist, orthodoxy.

My particular understanding of rationalism and the place of *a priori* knowledge needs some comment here. My feeling is that empiricism has dominated the intellectual scene for so long not simply because of its manifest and intrinsic merits, but rather because the champions of rationalism have presented something less than a united front. This has been compounded by the absence of a form of rationalism which can meet the demands of scientific materialism, and thus provide truly competitive explanations which are not instantly punctured by the merest whisper of the charge of metaphysical speculation. General *a priorism* is particularly vulnerable to this kind of criticism, especially if it is paired with an extreme coherence account of knowledge, with its self-refering explanatory basis. While Chomsky's revival of Leibnizian innatism has signalled an innovative approach in the field of linguistics, a general conflation of rationalism with innatism would expose the former to the dangers of solipcism. The type of rationalism that I have argued for is one which makes no claims about the innate capacities of the human mind, not does it posit any necessary truths about the world. Instead, the form of rationalism that I have adopted registers the important role that conceptual and (thus) discursive parameters play in social analysts' attempts to describe, characterise or explain features of the social world; features which clearly can be both a part of our experience of the world in which we live, and a part of a (material and ideal) world relatively independent of such experience, and in possession of its own distinct properties.

It is the intrinsic interdependence of rationalist and empiricist modes of knowledge, and the exact nature of this interdependence as I have described it, which ensures that the paradox between formal and concrete issues cannot be resolved in a biased or lopsided manner. Thus, the extreme *a priorism* of Winch's philosophical humanism has to be rejected along with the empirical scientific imperialism of philosophy's detractors amongst conventional sociologists. This realisation only accentuates the point that beneath the surface, both formal and substantive issues are informed by questions of an epistemological and ontological nature. Thus, these questions in themselves cannot be consigned by the sociological research community to some philosophical limbo-world where they are assumed to be applicable to a hermetically sealed universe and which are of only formal interest.

Possibly the most far-reaching insight of social scientific realism is that the social world (as opposed to the world of the science laboratory) is an open system. But this insight must be extended to its logical conclusion; if it is truly an open system then the discourses of social science interpenetrate each other to varying degrees, and in different ways. In the particular case of the underpinning of empirical or research questions by epistemological and ontological issues, it is of paramount importance that neither of these latter are views as self-evident by virtue of their assumed mutual escape from each other's influence. I have identified certain tendencies in both realist and cognate writing that appear to invite just such an interpretation. I have tried to point out the negative consequences of some of these tendencies by stressing the artifice of the visions they offer of the tasks of social science and the ensuring explanatory impoverishment engendered by them.

In my view, perhaps the core weakness of current realist writing is its elevation or privileging of ontological problems. My concern with the entire range of social scientific discourses, their stratified nature, and the importance of the empiricist-rationalist debate has been at the service of an attempt to rectify this assumption. The privileging of the ontological domain has taken several forms, but they all, in some way or other, bear upon the sorts of validity claims that realism licenses. The various forms have included a concern with the privileging of the empirically real as against the theoretically modelled elements of the social world; the assertion of practical rather than cognitive adequacy; the characterisation of the key problems of social analysis as ontological rather than epistemological; the search for causal mechanisms as opposed to acausal interdependencies; and the assertion of specific irreducible ontological features of the social world. My argument has been that it matters little which form (or conjunction of forms) such ontological privileging takes, they all produce a similar effect; that of constricting the explanatory scope and power of realism, and thus, of social science itself.

As a corollary to this, I have suggested that realism should not align itself with a wholesale rejection of objectivism in social analysis. The results of the exercise of such restraint would be that the integrity of the objectivist moments of social reality would be preserved and registered in our theories and descriptions of the social world. In this respect realism must break away from its predilections for, and residual commitments to, both phenomenological forms of reductionism, and to forms of analytic synthesis which, unwittingly, threaten to loosen our explanatory grip on the objective properties of social reality.

I have expressed my concern to widen the realm of possible objects of inquiry for realist social science primarily in terms of an extended view of social ontology, very much bearing in mind that this is informed by, and expressed in terms of, a fairly complex relation to epistemological matters. However, I have also expressed the 'extension of terms' in the form of two theses about the nature and functions of the language of social science. The first of these attempted to depict the different kinds or levels of social scientific language and their relation to the language of everyday life. The second thesis was logically entailed in the first, but had, nonetheless, a more immediate connection with the practical problems of qualitative field research. It is in such an area that the practical pay-off of philosophical concerns is most easily recognisable, but it is also this area which continues to present some formidable challenges to realism. Finally, as this last comment implies, I do not wish to claim that I have tackled (let alone solved) all the questions that I have raised in this book, but I do hope that my arguments will have some success in persuading those who are interested in the realist project that it is necessary to broaden its terms of reference in the specific ways I have indicated.

Appendix

The Philosophical Bogeyman: Misunderstanding the Relation between Theory and Method

When my article 'The Relation of Theory and Method: causal relatedness, historical contingency and beyond' appeared in the *Sociological Review* (1988) (and which appears in this book as part of chapter 4), it was followed by two critical responses in the same issue by Platt and Bulmer. In my opinion both of these responses seriously misrepresent and profoundly misunderstand my arguments. In what follows I identify the more salient of these misunderstandings and attempt to rectify them.

I will not dwell on all the points Platt deals with in response to my article because many of the points on which she claims I misrepresent her are rather pedantic, and I do not want to perpetuate a tedious (and potentially endless) argument about what was 'really meant'. Anyway, most of these minor points of difference are quite unimportant to my central arguments. My main concern was to use her discussion as a vehicle for my own thinking about realist (as opposed to conventional) interpretations of the relation between theory and method.

However, before getting to the major misunderstandings there are some gross misrepresentations of my own article which need to be cleared up. Platt repeats an accusation (point 1, p. 465 and point 4, p. 466) which both disfigures my original meaning and at the same time betrays an ignorance of material with which, at the time, I assumed readers in general might be familiar. On both these points Platt says that my assertion that survey analysis in general and *Gross et al's Explorations in Role Analysis* in particular display inattention to, or a disregard for, actors' meanings, is without foundation. In fact, she says, the reverse is the case on the basis that 'the focus of the whole study is on actors' expectations and definitions of the situation'! Of course, here I was referring to the well-rehearsed phenomenological critique of conventional (positivist) methods. At the time of writing my original article this seemed such an obvious and well-documented point that I did not think to repeat it. However, since it has led to such a gross misinterpretation by Platt I feel driven to elucidate further.

Of course, survey analyses including *Gross et al.* often focus on actors' 'expectations' and 'definitions of the situation' but the whole point of the phenomenological critique is that these are arrived at in a manner which denatures the emergent and dynamic character of social activity. The very notion of role in *Gross et al.*'s analysis is conceived of in a 'static' rather than a 'dynamic' way and depicts the relevant actors as empty-headed 'marionettes' who purportedly act according to the *researchers*' definitions of *their* expectations in a mechanical way. This is the brunt of Naegele's (1960) famous criticism of the (positivistic) scientism of Gross's study which speaks of human beings as if they were 'hollow-men'. The difference between

177

'positivist' versions of role theory as against 'interactionist' versions has been extensively documented (Keat and Urry 1973; Cicourel 1973; Turner 1962, 1985). The methodological differences between the survey analysis of actors' meanings, as impositions of researchers' meanings, or definitions 'by fiat' and the interactionist concern with actors' meanings has also been extensively analysed in Cicourel's *Method and Measurement in Sociology*. His contention is that fixed-choice questionnaire surveys impose deterministic grids on the possible responses of human actors and thus do not do justice to the emergent nature of actors' expectations and definitions. Nor do they reflect the problematic or situation-specific character of everyday life.

Platt (point 2, p.465) also twists my uncontentious statement that there is a 'compatibility' between survey research and hypothetico-deductive forms of theorising into the completely unfounded charge that I claim that hypothetico-deductive theorising is incompatible with experiments! I say nothing of the sort. In fact, I say the opposite on p. 458, stating that such theorising was shared not only by functionalists and non-functionalists but by psychologists and social psychologists. Surely it cannot have escaped Platt's notice that the *experimental* method has been dominant in psychology for some time now. Platt also accuses me of suggesting that surveys are *inevitably* accompanied by hypothetico-deductive forms of theorising. Again, I say nothing of the sort. What I do say is that they are commonly in each other's company. A world of difference I think.

Platt grossly misrepresents my arguments when she says (p. 466, point 3) that I 'assert a rational connection between functionalism and the survey' (Bulmer is also guilty of this error – see later comments). This interpretation is totally inconsistent with my whole thesis about a distinction between an implicate and explicate order. Platt clearly ignores my statement on p. 449 when I argue that there are no *necessary* rational connections between particular theoretical discourses and methods at an ontological level. The diagram at the top of the page indicates clearly that I include what I term methodological protocols (or research theory, an example of which is middle-range theory) at the ontological level. Indeed, this is why I say on p. 449 that '*In that sense and at that level* Platt is right to suggest that what rational connections do exist between theories and methods are ones of 'mere affinity' or 'tendencies to be associated'.

What I go on to say, and what Platt clearly confuses, is that this lack of rational connection at the ontological level does not preclude the indirect or submerged rational connections at the *epistemological* level. Platt may wish to think that I am asserting a simple rational connection between functionalism and the survey but in fact I am suggesting a much more subtle argument in which the distinctions between ontology and epistemology, and the implicate and explicate orders are of paramount importance.

A more charitable reading of my whole argument with careful attention to these pivotal distinctions might have averted such an outright misrepresentation of my argument. In connection with this, in her footnote (p. 469) Platt's statement that I *assume* 'that functionalism is compatible with *any* middle-range theory derived from particular data' (my emphasis), must be challenged on the grounds of its complete disregard for the truth of my actual arguments. I am at a loss to know how she arrives at this malignment, but since the footnote occurs in the context of the misrepresentation I have just dealt with, I assume that this erroneous assertion must be part of her general confusion over this point.

This misrepresentation is carried through into Platt's subsequent admission that she does not understand my general argument about 'rational connections' and this leads her again (p. 467) to repeat the same mistake about my arguments concerning the specific relation between functionalism and the survey. To properly understand the notion of rational connections one has to have some grasp of the philosophical debate between empiricism and rationalism. For reasons of restricted space I had to condense my argument in the *Sociological Review*, and assumed the reader's familiarity with certain debates. The confusion about the term 'rationalism' is well evidenced in Platt's use of the term 'irrationality' (p. 468) as an implied 'counter' to rationalism. As I noted in chapters 2 and 3 of this book, there are various technical usages and meanings of the term rationalism (including general *a priorism*, innatism and necessitarianism), but none of these *theories of knowledge* (that is, explanations of the nature, scope and origins of knowledge), must be confused with non-technical (that is non-epistemological) usages which refer to a person's actions or behaviour as being 'rational' as opposed to 'irrational'.

I find Platt's arguments on p. 468 at best obscure, but at one point she does impute to me a patently erroneous position when she says that I appear to think that ideas have people, rather than people having ideas. I cannot in all honesty, fathom the logical basis for this assertion; similarly, I am at a loss to find any evidence in my article which even remotely suggests that I would believe such an absurdity. Again, I think her confusion must arise from her incorrect conflation of rationalism as a theory of knowledge, and the rationality or irrationality of people's behaviour. Of course, people (and researchers in particular) acquire ideas through social influence; it *is* people who have ideas. But where do they come from? My answer is that they come from prevailing climates of 'social influence' and they get modified or changed through people imagining and trying out alternative possibilities. But this does not alter the fact that general bodies of ideas in themselves have a relative independence from particular instances of practice. Rational interlocks occur at the level of the conceptual integration of clustering of such bodies of ideas (including 'theories'; see Hesse 1974, Thomas 1979).

Again, Platt completely ignores the totality and subtlety of my argument by claiming, quite fallaciously, that I assume that rational connections are 'automatically translated into practice', . . . 'because of the rationality'. I say no such thing nor imply any such thing. What I do is challenge her assertion that what actors say they are doing is the most reliable way of evaluating their practice and to use this as seemingly incontrovertible evidence for the absence of a link of any kind (epistemological or empirical) between functionalism and the survey. Here she ignores a whole chunk of my argument on p. 455–6 which discusses why actors' accounts may not be reliable (Platt does not even appear to conceive of this as a possibility), and therefore must be supplemented by analysis of epistemological commitments that are contained in their work and research practices.

So to Bulmer's piece. He begins by saying that his major disagreement is with my assertion that specific methods 'are always saturated with theoretical assumptions'. He then proceeds to say (if it was logically entailed in my assertion, which it quite patently is not) that there is 'no necessary connection between the use of a particular method and a particular methodological standpoint'. This is exactly the same mistake as Platt. Bulmer has not taken into consideration the central distinction I make between epistemological and ontological elements, nor between the implicate and explicate orders. I'm afraid I have to point out once again that I do *not* make the claim imputed to me by Bulmer, and thus, the same comments I made in relation to Platt's fallacious claims about my 'asserting a rational connection between functionalism and the survey' apply equally to Bulmer.

It is instructive to note that Bulmer's 'central disagreement' about theory saturation of methods is transposed into the principal contradiction in his later comments. On p. 472 he states 'it would be more plausible to argue that the most fundamental characteristic of empirical sociological enquiry is its embeddedness in theory'. Not only does Bulmer speak of this 'revelation' as if it were his unique discovery (which it is not), but he seems blissfully unaware that the statement is entirely consonant with the theory saturation of methods that I argue for, and which he insists he disagrees with. I fear he must be disagreeing with himself for otherwise he would have to commit himself to the absurd position that acquiring and looking through the lens of a particular method magically obliterates the 'theory embeddedness' of 'empirical sociological inquiry'.

If I may be permitted a *soupçon* of immodesty I do feel that my article goes well beyond these sorts of bland assertions of theory-ladenness, by trying to specify in some detail the exact nature of certain aspects of this problem. Not the least of these is trying to unpack the variant meanings, levels and functions of *theoretical* presuppositions, which both Platt and Bulmer seem to view, wrongly in my opinion, as entirely unproblematic. Also, Bulmer's view that I say 'very little about the problematic relationship between theory and evidence' seems rather arrogant in the light of what I take to be the quite modest intention of my article, which was to clear some of the necessary ground-work for tackling this problem.

Bulmer's second disagreement is in the form of a quaint but sermonising lecture on my supposed misuse of the term empiricism. Here Bulmer demonstrates a lack of understanding of the philosophical debate between empiricism and rationalism. Anyone familiar with this debate would be aware that there are various forms of empiricism just as there are of rationalism. In this book, as in other work (1985, 1986) I employ a distinction between naive and sophisticated empiricism, and while I would not claim that this exhausts the possibilities, it certainly goes beyond Bulmer's complacent and bland assumption that empiricism *per se* has been banished simply because social scientists have finally woken up to the myth of theory-neutral observation and data. Bulmer appears to be entirely ignorant of the fact that the debate is no longer (and has never been in philosophical circles), whether or not empiricism (in whatever form) does or does not exist; it is, rather about the respective truth claims of empiricism in relation to rationalism (a topic which has been treated in great detail throughout this book.)

The sad truth of the 'let us get to the facts and forget about the philosophical speculation' school of thought which Bulmer represents, is that it perpetuates the state of ignorance and naivete from which it stems. There are two common and pernicious mistakes which result from this line of thought. The first is that the kind of arguments I have set forth are in *direct competition* with historical or empirical analysis in general. There is nothing in my article which justifies such wild misrepresentation. My intention in this respect is clear throughout; that this kind of philosophical analysis and historical/empirical research are complementary, with two important caveats. First, that the relationship between them is a complex one and second that the historical/empirical dimension is neither privileged nor autonomous.

The second pernicious and scare-mongering tactic typical of the 'philosophy is a bogeyman' school is the one employed by Bulmer (p. 471–7) in accusing me of adopting a position which insists on what amounts to an extreme coherence theory of truth which denies the validity of an external empirical object world against which certain theories, hypotheses or statements can be checked or validated. I have always vehemently opposed the extreme coherence theory and the arguments in this book simply reinforce this claim. What I have tried to do is avoid the dismissal of all forms of coherence theory by the dogmatic assertion of naive correspondence theories and simplistic falsificationist schemas which do not do justice to the diversity of phenomena subject to social inquiry and to the diversity of explanatory forms and methods of inquiry that exist in the practices of social scientists today – uncomfortable as this may be to those of Bulmer's ilk.

This brings me to the final point. Bulmer accuses me of 'destructive' and 'pernicious' tendencies because he claims, (quite wrongly), that I contribute to 'a sociological Babel' which, in turn, is connected with 'the relatively poor scholarly and academic standing of sociology in Britain's wider intellectual community'. What a spectacular own-goal! Bulmer appears entirely unaware of the nature and importance of particular theoretical and philosophical issues! But the witch-hunt element is clear here. Bulmer's hysterical tirade is meant to be a warning (fatuous as this may be) that if you do not think like 'us', then 'we' will have to try to discredit your ideas by contorting them beyond recognition.

But I do sympathise with the 'little-boy-lost' element of Bulmer's hyperdefensiveness. It reminds me of the Peter Pan wish to remain in a perpetual child-like state which provides comforting support to all the naive myths about the real grown-up world of uncertainty, ambiguity and complexity. Let us keep it simple, let us close our eyes and imagine the world is the way we would wish it to be. Let us pretend that the unsettling and perhaps frightening complexity of reality does not exist, then we can live in a continuous state of self-delusion. In this respect the most pernicious element of Bulmer's fears and defensiveness is that they are expressed in a professional journal as a form of *attack* on constructive dialogue and freedom of thought.

Anyone who could realistically claim to know anything about the nature of my work thus far should not have failed to notice that my intention has always been to strengthen the empirical and methodological basis of sociology by tackling problems (such as the nature of theoretical presuppositions and their effects on different levels of practice) to which many, like Bulmer, have turned a blind-eye. The whole thrust of my work has been to uproot the dogmatic assertions of closed-minded defenders of 'orthodoxy' whatever its forms. A corollary of this has been an effort to expose the wooliness of thinking and utter complacency of those who wish to suppress certain forms of inquiry and to close down the possibilities of interdisciplinary dialogue and co-operation.

References

Althusser, L., *For Marx* (London: Allen Lane, 1969).

Ashton *et al.*, 'The Determinants of Young Adults' Labour Market Status' (E S R C Report, 1989).

Ayer, F., *Language, Truth & Logic* (Harmondsworth: Penguin, 1971).

Barbalet, J., 'Power, Structural Resources, and Agency', *Current Perspectives in Social Theory* 8 (1987) pp. I–24.

Becker, H., *Sociological Work* (Chicago: Aldine, 1970).

Benson, D., 'A Revolution in Sociology', *Sociology* 8 (1974) pp. 125–9.

Benton, T., *The Philosophical Foundations of the Three Sociologies* (London: Routledge, 1977).

Benton, T., 'Realism and Social Science', *Radical Philosophy* 27 (1981) pp. 13–21.

Berger, P. and Luckmann, T., *The Social Construction of Reality* (Harmondsworth: Penguin, 1971).

Bhaskar, R., *The Possibility of Naturalism* (Brighton: Harvester, 1979).

Blumer, H., 'Sociological Analysis and the Variable', *American Sociological Review*, xxi (1956) pp. 683–90.

Blumer, H., *Symbolic Interactionism* (New Jersey: Prentice-Hall, 1969).

Bohm, D., *Wholeness and the Implicate Order* (London: Ark, 1981).

Bourdieu, P., *Outline of a Theory of Practice* (Cambridge: University Press, 1977).

Braverman, H., *Labour and Monopoly Capital* (New York: 1974).

Bruyn, S., *The Human Perspective in Sociology* (New Jersey: Prentice-Hall, 1966).

Bulmer, M., 'A Comment on: The Relation of Theory and Method: Causal Relatedness, Historical Contingency and Beyond', *Sociological Review* 36 (1988) pp. 470–3.

Burawoy, M., *Manufacturing Consent* (Chicago: University of Chicago Press, 1979).

Cicourel, A., *Method and Measurement in Sociology* (New York: Free Press, 1964).

Cicourel, A., *Cognitive Sociology* (Harmondsworth: Penguin, 1973).

Collins, R., 'On the Micro-Foundations of Macro-Sociology', *American Journal of Sociology* 86 (1981) pp. 984–1014.

Cottingham, J., *Rationalism* (London: Palladin, 1984).

Douglas, J. (ed.) *Understanding Everyday Life* (London: Routledge, 1971).

Douglas, J., *Existential Sociology* (Cambridge: Cambridge University Press, 1977).

Durkheim, E., *The Rules of Sociological Method* (London: Macmillan, 1982).

Edwards, R., *Contested Terrain* (London: Heinemann, 1979).

Elias, N., *What is Sociology?* (London: Hutchinson, 1978).

Feyerabend, P., *Against Method* (London: New Left Books, 1975).

184   *References*

Garfinkel, H., *Studies in Ethnomethodology* (New Jersey: Prentice-Hall, 1967).
Giddens, A., *New Rules of Sociological Method* (London: Hutchinson, 1976).
Giddens, A., *Central Problems in Social Theory* (London: Macmillan, 1979).
Giddens, A., *The Constitution of Society* (Cambridge: Polity, 1984).
Giddens, A., *Modern Social Theory* (Cambridge: Polity, 1986).
Glaser, B. and Strauss, A., *Awareness of Dying* (Chicago: Aldine, 1965).
Glaser, B. and Strauss, A., *The Discovery of Grounded Theory* (Chicago: Aldine, 1967).
Gross, N. *et al.*, *Explorations in Role Analysis: Studies of the School Superintendency Role* (New York: Wiley, 1958).
Harré, R., *Social Being* (Oxford: Blackwell, 1979).
Harré, R., 'Philosophical aspects of the micro-macro problem', in K. Knorr-Cetina and A. Cicourel (eds), *Advances in Social Theory and Methodology* (London: Routledge, 1981) pp. 139–60.
Harré, R. and Secord, P., *The Explanation of Social Behaviour* (Oxford: Blackwell, 1972).
Hesse, M., *The Structure of Scientific Inference* (London: Macmillan, 1974).
Hindess, B. and Hirst, P., *Mode of Production and Social Formation* (London: Macmillan, 1977).
Keat, R., 'Positivism, Naturalism and Anti-Naturalism in the Social Sciences', *Journal for the Theory of Social Behaviour* I (1971) pp. 3–17.
Keat, R and Urry, J., *Social Theory as Science* (London: Routledge, 1975).
Knorr-Cetina, K., 'The micro-sociological challenge of macro-sociology: towards a reconstruction of social theory and methodology' in K. Knorr-Cetina and A. Cicourel (eds), *Advances in Social Theory and Methodology* (London: Routledge, 1981) pp. 1–47.
Krekel, R., 'Unequal Opportunity Structure and Labour Market Segmentation', *Sociology* 14 (1980) pp. 525–49.
Kuhn, T., *The Structure of Scientific Revolutions* (Chicago: University Press, 1962).
Lakatos. I., 'Falsification and the Methodology of Scientific Research Programmes', in I. Lakatos and A. Musgrave (eds), *Criticism and the Growth of Knowledge* (Cambridge: Cambridge University Press, 1970).
Laing, R. and Esterson, A., *Sanity, Madness and the Family*(London: Tavistock, 1964).
Layder, D., *Occupational Careers in Contemporary Britain: With special reference to the Acting Profession* (unpublished PhD Thesis, London School of Economics, 1976).
Layder, D., *Structure, Interaction and Social Theory* (London: Routledge, 1981).
Layder, D., 'Grounded Theory: A Constructive Critique', *Journal for the Theory of Social Behaviour* 12 (1982), pp 103–23.
Layder, D., 'Sources and Levels of Commitment in Actors' Careers', *Work and Occupations* 11 (1984) pp. 147–62.
Layder, D., 'Power, Structure and Agency', *Journal for the Theory of Social Behaviour* 15 (1985a) pp. 131–49.

Layder, D., 'Beyond Empiricism: The Promise of Realism', *Philosophy of the Social Sciences* 15 (1985b) pp. 255–74.

Layder, D., 'Social Reality as Figuration: A Critique of Elias's Conception of Sociological Analysis', *Sociology* 20 (1986) pp. 367–86.

Layder, D., 'Key Issues in Structuration Theory', *Current Perspectives in Social Theory* 8 (1987) pp. 25–46.

Layder, D., 'The Relation of Theory and Method: Causal Relatedness, Historical Contingency and Beyond', *Sociological Review* 36 (1988) pp. 441–63.

Layder, D., 'The Macro – Micro Distinction, Social Relations and Methodological Bracketing', *Current Perspectives in Social Theory* 9 (1988).

Lemert, E., 'Paranoia and the Dynamics of Exclusion', *Sociometry* 25 (1962) pp. 2–20.

Louch, A., *Explanation and Human Action* (Oxford: Blackwell, 1966).

Lukes, S., *Essays in Social Theory* (London: Macmillan, 1977).

Manicas, P. and Secord, P., 'The Implications for Psychology of the New Philosophy of Science', *American Psychologist* 38 (1983) pp. 399–413.

Mead, G., *Mind, Self and Society* (Chicago: University of Chicago Press, 1967).

Merton, R., *Social Theory and Social Structure* (Illinois: Free Press, 1968).

Naegele, K., 'Superintendency versus Superintendents: A Critical Essay', *Harvard Educational Review*, 1960.

Pateman, T., *Language in Mind and Language in Society* (Oxford: Clarendon Press, 1987).

Platt, J., 'Functionalism and the Survey: the relation of theory and method', *The Sociological Review* 34 (1986) pp. 501–36.

Platt, J., 'Comment on: The relation of theory and method: Causal relatedness, historical contingency and beyond', *Sociological Review* 36 (1988) pp. 464–9.

Popper, K., *The Logic of Scientific Discovery* (London: Hutchinson, 1959).

Popper, K., *Objective Knowledge: An Evolutionary Approach* (Oxford: Clarendon, 1972).

Poulantzas, N., *Political Power and Social Classes* (London: New Left Books, 1973).

Roche, M., *Phenomenology, Language and the Social Sciences* (London: Routledge, 1973).

Rock, P., *The Making of Symbolic Interactionism* (London: Macmillan, 1979).

Rosenberg, M., *Occupations and Values* (Illinois: Free Press, 1957).

Rowe, D., *The Experience of Depression* (Chichester: Wiley, 1978).

Rowe, D., *Depression: The Way Out of Your Prison* (London: Routledge, 1983).

Sartre, J-P., *Being and Nothingness: An Essay in Phenomenological Ontology* (New York: Washington Square Press, 1966).

Sayer, A., *Method in Social Science* (London: Hutchinson, 1984).

Sayer, D., *Marx's Method: Science and Critique in Capital* (Hassocks: Harvester, 1979).

Schutz, A., *Collected Papers* (The Hague: Mouton, 1967).

186   *References*

Sofer, C., *Men in Mid-Career* (Cambridge: Cambridge University Press, 1970).
Stryker, S., *Symbolic Interactionism: A Social Structural Version* (New Jersey: Prentice-Hall, 1981).
Thomas, D., *Naturalism and Social Science* (Cambridge: University Press, 1979).
Turner, R., 'Role-Taking: Process versus Conformity' in A. Rose (ed.), Human Behaviour and Social Processes (Boston: Houghton Mifflin, 1962).
Turner, R., 'The Convergence Between Structuralist and Interactionist Role Theories', in H. Helle and S. Eisenstadt (eds), *Micro-Sociological Theory: Perspectives on Sociological Theory* (London: Sage) pp. 22–36.
Van Fraasen, Bas C., *The Scientific Image* (Oxford: Clarendon Press, 1980).
Weber, M., *The Theory of Economic and Social Organization* (New York: Free Press, 1964).
Whorf, B., *Language, Thought and Reality* (Boston: Wiley, 1959).
Willer, D. and J., *Systematic Empiricism: A Critique of a Pseudo-Science* (New Jersey: Prentice-Hall, 1973).
Winch, P., *The Idea of a Social Science* (London: Routledge, 1963).
Wilson, J., 'Realist Philosophy as a Foundation For Marxian Social Theory', *Current Perspectives in Social Theory* 3 (1982) pp. 243–63.
Wright, E., *Class Structure and Income Determination* (New York: Academic Press, 1979).

Index